e-customer

There is a new world which we can look at but we cannot see. Yet within it, the forces of technology and imagination are overturning the way we work and the way we do business. ft.com is both gateway and guide to this world. We understand it because we are part of it. But we also understand the needs of businesses which are taking their first steps into it, and those still standing hesitantly on the threshold. Above all, we understand that, as with all business challenges, the key to success lies not with the technology itself, but with the people who must use it and manage it. People like you.

See the world. Visit us at www.ft.com today.

e-customer

customers just got
faster and smarter.
catch up.

Max Mckeown

FINANCIAL TIMES

Prentice Hall

An imprint of **Pearson Education**

London · New York · San Francisco · Toronto · Sydney
Tokyo · Singapore · Hong Kong · Cape Town · Madrid
Paris · Milan · Munich · Amsterdam

PEARSON EDUCATION LIMITED

Head Office:
Edinburgh Gate
Harlow CM20 2JE
Tel: +44 (0)1279 623623
Fax: +44 (0)1279 431059

London Office:
128 Long Acre, London WC2E 9AN
Tel: +44 (0)207 447 2000
Fax: +44 (0)207 240 5771
Website: www.business-minds.com

—————————————————————

First published in Great Britain in 2001

ISBN 0 273 65020 3

British Library Cataloguing in Publication Data
A CIP catalogue record for this book can be obtained from the British Library

10 9 8 7 6 5 4 3 2 1

Designed by Claire Brodmann Book Designs, Lichfield, Staffs
Typeset by Pantek Arts Ltd, Maidstone, Kent
Printed and bound in Great Britain by Redwood Books, Trowbridge

The Publishers' policy is to use paper manufactured from sustainable forests.

For Deborah

As you wish.

about the author

Max Mckeown has been described as a 'new media business architect', finding ways of exploiting new trends to the benefit of all company stakeholders, including customers and employees. He is a business writer and strategy consultant to organizations across industry sectors. He is founder and chairman of Maverick & Strong, a company that specializes in rebuilding organizations around their customers. He is also a popular conference speaker and a regular magazine columnist.

He started his customer contact apprenticeship with First Direct (telephone banking pioneers), developed leading edge e-solutions with AIT (innovative software house responsible for the legendary Keybank and Woolwich multi-channel systems), helped found the CRM group with CMG (largest European Systems Integrator), joined C3 (Customer Contact Company) before founding Maverick & Strong. He is currently strategic advisor for a number of global e-business ventures.

Destroy apathy, create value. Join him at www.maxmckeown.com

'After 15 years working with US Presidents. My advice?
Listen to Max Mckeown.
On the wisdom scale, he is a cross between Buddha and Bill Gates.'

Mary Spillane, author of
Branding Yourself!

contents

foreword

A word to the wise
Customers will never go out of fashion.

WAP will go out of fashion. Personal computers will become landfill site material. Interactive Digital Television will lose and then regain its sparkle. Technologies with wild, wacky, and unpronounceable names will arrive and depart unmourned. Each device will have frenzies and crises.

All these things and more will happen but in 50 years people will still be shopping: at least they will still have needs to be met through an exchange of value. This will remain a constant.

But the services must change. The stuff has to improve. The e-customer is evolving.[1] His aspirations have been fed by years of science fiction and soap-style images of the rich and famous. He has been promised more. He is certain that a better everything is out there.

The only way to get the e-customer's cash is to create stuff that has value for him. You need to understand him. You need to get closer. You and your colleagues must learn to empathize, visualize and innovate on behalf of the e-customer.

That's why this book is not focused on presenting long structured case studies. In such material you only learn what your competitors want you to learn about their services. You don't think they would let you in on anything of real value do you?

Perhaps their success is not success at all. Perhaps it won't keep them alive, thriving, enjoying the benefits of growth. Perhaps they have only transferred their off-line products and services online in the most mindless, uncreative manner – with no value added for the hundreds of millions invested.

The focus here is about competing for the attention and spending power of the wired generation You can't do that by just reading accounts of what others have done. A set of principles is needed so that you can create your own innovation – so that you can win the mind and wallet of the e-customer.

Technologists talk about 'best of breed' as the ideal mixture of components, collected from different manufacturers, in order to do a required job. The examples that are presented in this book may not be perfect. In fact they are not perfect. So look on them as springboards to your own innovations. If you can't improve on them and can only copy then you will only ever be in defensive mode anyway. Grab hold of them and ask how you can slot together enough of these best of breed approaches into one world beating e-customer inspired organization. Underline what you find useful. Make your own lists. Do your own work. Create your own differentiated benefit to the e-customer by opening up a dialogue with him.

Creating useful stuff for the e-customer will never go out of fashion.

The
Situ

IMPOSSIBLE
IMF
MISSION FORCE

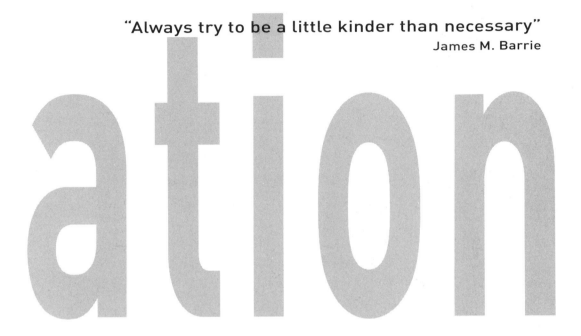

"Always try to be a little kinder than necessary"

James M. Barrie

It's the customer, stupid

The stress of millennium life in the economic first world comes not from too little but from too much. It is the blessing and curse of our generation. We have to work harder so that we can afford to play harder because we desire the lifestyles that Hollywood promises.

The need to put in more effort to enjoy more leisure is at the heart of the e-customer profile. But despite what has become the 'cash rich, time poor' cliché, the e-customer is still more often offered the chance to 'save money' with internet companies than the chance to 'save time' or 'improve your lifestyle'.

Companies witlessly rush to market with offerings that do not consider the demands and requirements of their e-customers. They put forward services that seem to judge the e-customer to be an unthinking consumer – an undiscerning diner, a muncher of mediocre meals.

Is the e-customer ready simply to eat what is laid out before him? Not at all certain. He does not have an automatic appetite. The gadget junkies will keep buying, unable (and unwilling) to stop. The stuff is enough for them. It doesn't necessarily have to deliver better lives, it just has to look pretty and have flashing lights in all the right places.

The much tougher group is the wider population of potential and actual e-customers. Some of them don't always see the point at all. Others want to have the advantages made clear and unambiguous. They both need to be enticed in, educated. And most of all they want services that really deliver.

Services that deliver. Deliver what? What the e-customer appreciates. What he wants to pay for. Not just a simple set of objective improvements, but stuff that speaks his language, pushes his buttons, clicks with his karma and, most importantly, fits in with his priorities.

" Services that deliver.
Deliver what?
What the e-customer appreciates "

And what are these priorities? Just listen to the experience of self-titled 'personal coach' Cheryl Richardson. She has created a new profession out of simply helping the e-customer to make better decisions about their over-busy lives.

MORE AND MORE PEOPLE ARE TIRED OF **THE FAST-PACED, FRENZIED** 'INFORMATION AGE' AND ARE INTERESTED IN **HIGHER-QUALITY** LIVES – LIVES IN WHICH THEY HAVE **MORE TIME FOR THEMSELVES** AND THEIR RELATIONSHIPS, **MORE ENERGY** TO INVEST IN THEIR EMOTIONAL, PHYSICAL, AND SPIRITUAL **WELL-BEING.**

WHETHER YOU'RE A **CORPORATE EXECUTIVE** WORKING **60 HOURS A WEEK,** A **SINGLE PARENT** TRYING TO RAISE A FAMILY, OR SOMEONE WHO'S **TIRED OF** **FEELING** STRESSED OUT AND PRESSED FOR TIME, **YOU HAVE A CHOICE** ABOUT HOW TO LIVE YOUR LIFE.

Her book, *Take Time for Your Life*,[2] is a huge best-seller. Tens of thousands bought it. More than 40 million people in the USA alone buy anti-stress and self-improvement books every year. The e-customer is trying hard to tell the producers and providers of stuff everywhere that he wants more life for his lira.

Simply delivering products cheaper to the customer's door isn't very creative. It may be logistically challenging to many businesses involved, but it isn't likely to thrill the e-customer. Sometimes he isn't sure what all the fuss is about. Usually he just expects more.

If he spares it any thought at all he wonders just how hard it can be to turn his self-typed order into a rapid delivery. He does all the work, so of course he deserves the price savings. This is what he has been taught to think. He wanted to think it anyway. But we have advertised and marketed the savings angle so hard that he accepts it as his birthright.

If you sell it cheap you have to make it for less. Cheaper requires greater efficiency. Or poverty. And penniless does not make good shareholder reading. Less money at just the time that the business requires more investment to make the services really work – it's a tough combination. And it has been accentuated by so much of the spending on marketing. Spend more: to tell your e-customers that they can save more. Are you sure that is the most sensible approach?

Check your money-grabbing motivations in at the door

Inventiveness, experimentation, greed and fear: the driving forces behind so much of the activity. Inventors produce tools. Experimenters play with them and find that they might just be able to compete with the big guys. Greed drives the flocks of net millionaire 'wannabees' to launch copy-cat services. Fear provokes the established businesses to invest in fending off the start-ups.

Businesses globally continue to pour in money. The cost of the infrastructure to support such services is immense. The investment required to provide the services themselves is even higher. Those who have paid in want to see pay-back, a rapid return on the investment of millions or billions.

Bidding for the 'thin air' licences required for new generation, high performance wireless communications has led to phenomenal prices being paid. And now the proud owners of such licences need to build the networks to utilize them. They will have to come up with reasons for the e-customer to pay more than $1,000 a head for the new services.

The Iridium bankruptcy of March 2000 demonstrates that technology advances are not enough to energize the e-customer. It demanded $1,200 for a satellite phone with the single proposition that:

THERE'LL BE NOWHERE TO HIDE.

YOUR BOSS WILL BE ABLE TO REACH YOU
IN THE AMAZON; YOUR FAMILY CAN GET IN TOUCH
IF YOU'RE IN THE **ANTARCTIC.**

The e-customer did not rush to participate, despite Iridium's stunning technical achievement of launching a worldwide mobile phone service complete with its own set of 66 low orbiting satellites. Iridium failed to answer the question 'why?'. It did not bring any significant improvements in the lifestyles of its e-customers.

Eventually everyone will simply be shunted over on to the new technologies, as older technologies are taken off-line and discontinued. The weight of existing businesses involved will press the e-customer into using and paying for the infrastructure. It could be done by simply increasing prices for those using existing services, or by phasing those services out and replacing them with new, faster, more expensive options. Either way it will have to be done rapidly to avoid cash difficulties for the companies involved.

Non-technology products and service companies face other more finely balanced questions. They have already invested in certain electronic channels. They have staked a great deal on their success but may now need to throw more into the pot before winning the hand.

For many, fear was the main driver behind massive or minor investment in new electronic channels. Fear of competition – what they *might* do, what they have just announced. Fear of being left behind. Fear of their own ignorance.

"The trick

focused on the lifestyle of the e-customer

It is fear that has led them to commit their future into the minds and hands of consultancies. Fear that has made them launch services without profit objectives. Fear that has sometimes encouraged them to cut out the healthy internet flesh from the ageing existing business.

They don't know what to do with all this new technology so they choose to ignore it, treat it lavishly, or relinquish it completely.

Many companies actually cut out their own experimenters and inventors – the source of creativity. And it is from here that the value is born: between the inventor and the e-customer. The trick is ensuring that the inventiveness is focused on the lifestyle of the e-customer so that it will return sufficient cash to allow business to continue and improve.

Some electronic channel companies have already failed, despite the dramatic growth of their potential market. Why? One reason is the number of internet and related plans that plot immense growth rates for the internet market and base their own growth on capturing a growing percentage of that market.

is ensuring that inventiveness is

so that it will return

sufficient cash to allow

business to continue and improve **"**

The inventive do not need to focus on the statistics.[3] The difficulty
with them anyway is that they can be, and most often are, abused.
More important are enduring principles that can guide and shape the
design of stuff that the e-customer will want to use, buy and value.[4]

Forget detailed statistical modelling

There are just so many estimates and forecasts about how many
internet users there will be, about how many mobile phone users there
will be, about how much money they will spend. This need not
concern you too much. The key to designing attractive stuff for the
e-customer is to build that which (in his opinion) will make his life
better.

The general size of the market is not as important as the size of your
market. The market is large enough to be viable. There are hundreds of
millions of potential and actual e-customers already. If you launch
something of interest to them they will come in a 'Fields of

Dreams[5] way. Look at the way the phenomenon of the dancing hamsters[6] shot around the virtual world. Suddenly they appeared on computers everywhere and even escaped into the real world to release a hit record. Did anyone there do detailed statistical modelling to formulate those little creations? No they did not!

dancing hamsters

Similarly, the makers of Pokémon, a product of the e-customer age, did not consider how to take their slice of the established market for trading little pocket monsters. Instead they thought, 'Children. What are they like? What do they do? Bet they would love something that combines trading, competing, fantasy and fighting!' Of course they did market research but that was after they had the BIG idea.

For every piece of e-stuff that hits the big time there are millions of pieces that are ignored. And anyone that is launching into the great, scary e-world as part of their full-time job or using a significant proportion of their savings wants to be certain of success.

You don't want to be one of the honourable losers! Well, it is possible to tread a defensive, copy-cat path into the domain of the e-customer but that does not mean it is safe or guaranteed. In order to attempt even this you will still need to be fully informed about the activities and plans of the competition. You will need to know what they are doing so that you can launch replica services. You will need to ensure that you are never so far behind them that they build an insurmountable advantage over you.

After all your efforts and despite all your investment, you should be aware that the internet has lowered the normal geographic, demographic and economic barriers that have kept you in business up to now. Even allowing for the difficulties in building physical supply chains to support virtual channels it has still become easier. The world of 'outsourced everything' will soon reduce this barrier further.

Thinking otherwise is to join those people who assumed that the train would never come to town because the tracks didn't run that far!

An increase in the number of suppliers in the market selling the same product will lead to greater choice. You will find yourself somewhere on a much bigger list. Number 8 in your market in size may translate into number 72 in the world. Number 2 in terms of quality may become number 284. It's like being the best soccer player in the USA and finding yourself in the World Cup. And we know what happened there.[7]

Faced with this scenario, some businesses will be bought or merged to reduce supply. Some will choose to 'give up' the fight for the mind of the e-customer by providing services or products to other more significant players in the market. These options are not fun, or exciting or motivational. They will rarely return increased shareholder value because they are not based on increasing the value of the company's assets.

An alternative is to actually do something **new**. To experience the pleasures of **organic growth** based on providing something that is valued by the e-customer that you serve. Aha! That really would be different.

But what have many businesses chosen to do with the growth potential? They either do exactly what they have been doing but do it via the internet. Or, if their use of the internet is even the slightest bit innovative, they spin it off into a separate business – so removing their core company from the source of energy, the corporate elixir of life. This doesn't make much sense but you have to understand that people always try to hide away what they do not understand.

Find out what the e-customer wants

Don't find out what e-customers buy now. Find out about what they want from their lives. Find out what they hate about your services and about those of your competitors. Find out their favourite ways of spending time. Come up with new stuff and then try it out with colleagues, friends, family and e-customers. Don't expect them to say that they like what you are showing to them at first if it is new. The newer it is the harder it may be to explain. But keep trying until you understand what the key advertising messages need to be – until you know what the e-customer values in relation to what you are offering.

The testing does not even have to be high-tech. The creator of the Palm Pilot, one of the greatest inventions for the e-customer to date, just cut out a piece of wood, stuck it in his pocket and carried it around with him. Whenever he needed an address or a diary date, he would take it out and follow the steps that his design stipulated. If it took too long or was too much hassle, he simply redesigned.

Your testing can follow similar lines *before involving* the cost and constraints of a full-blown IT project. Story-boarding and concept walk-throughs are not new techniques but they are vital. And they may be completely new and even alien to you, your company and your suppliers.

This kind of e-customer testing is seldom carried out because many internet companies are so busy with the project, the partnerships and the process that they forget to focus on the e-customer. In effect they are busy talking to the delivery boy or concentrating on stacking shelves rather than giving eye contact and the correct change to the e-customer. This is bad business. And in an industry that needs to establish customer loyalty it is a disaster.

It is all the more necessary because business plans can often be written by the guy or gal who knows most about the internet in a particular company but has little grasp of business models, marketing, operations, or customers. Alternatively, the driving force behind a new internet initiative can be a greedy or naive visionary who wants to be part of the 'next big thing' but knows very little about any of its component parts.

So what happens? The more convincing or well connected the individual or group that is driving the internet the more cash and goodwill they are able to obtain. This is rarely proportionate to the knowledge that individual or group has about the internet. Their knowledge only needs to seem impressive to investors whose knowledge is equally or obviously deficient.

Just ask yourself how much internet business knowledge can there be when 75% of people that use it have less than two years experience with it. This level of experience reduces yet further in the group who are responsible for many of these investment decisions.

Cash is obtained with promises of dramatic growth and price-led competitiveness made possible 'in the long term' by reductions in operational costs. E-customers will be seduced by low prices and then turned into loyal, repeat buyers through an ill-defined and mysterious process.

Keep your e-customer interested

The evidence is that e-commerce will not continue to keep pace with web usage itself unless the e-customer is engaged in the process. Slow-downs should be expected as people buy their computers, get online for the first time, buy something but are then not sufficiently motivated to keep buying.

If the e-customer is let down once or twice their natural distrust will take over. There are more worthwhile uses of time on and off-line than an unreliable, dull, illogical and protracted purchasing process.[8]

There is always another site just beyond the next hyperlink. The e-customer can log out, search for something better, or return to old favourites. In a world of 6.5 million different dot.com domains and millions more channels he will never run out of places to be, instead of with you.[9]

As many as 75% of people give up filling in the application forms before buying. On many corporate sites the stay on the home page is only three or four seconds. And the stay on the whole site in general is not much longer.

It is only by keeping your e-customer interested that you will make them purchase. Only by fulfilling your promises and their expectations that they will remain loyal. Only by having loyal e-customers that you can make them into profitable e-customers.

How much is an e-customer worth? You could look at lifetime value – the number of purchases that he will make from their first credit card to their last dying wish. Then figure out what percentage of this spending is on stuff that you provide.

That's the maximum lifetime value of each e-customer. It's a fun number. It makes you dream of money and salute the stars and stripes even if you are not American. US citizens can move directly to worship mode.

If you can get the potential value into the heads of your team it will help. They will start to see walking, talking, e-mailing stacks of cash. We are preconditioned not to turn down money and gift horses, so we will also find it hard to be rude to personified lucre. And as long as your e-customers wash, it isn't even filthy lucre.

Earning money from your e-customer

Next is the sad part. It involves figuring out what proportion of the lifetime value e-customers are likely to spend with you each month so that you can determine how much you can afford to spend on them over the same period.

"How much is an

Obviously you can 'invest' by spending now what you hope to get back much later. Be careful not to confuse investing with throwing a good party in the hope that your friends (e-customers) will stick around. It is best to avoid a prodigal dot.com scenario. What you need to do is find some real friends. Keep between the stingy and the extravagant extremes.

If your numbers look too low you have a problem. And especially if they look lower than your start-up and fixed costs then something has to change. Sometimes the change comes through altering key parts of the business model. Business models are just the way that you earn your money.

A clue for you. Earning money does not have to follow a simple purchase and payment scheme. There have always been alternatives and the internet has made them far more accessible and flexible.

There's the **Eyeball model**. Get paid for promoting other people's stuff. It's like a mixture between commission-only sales and leaflet posting and if you have something others find interesting then it's a great way of being rewarded. If you get it right you get super-champion rewards.

You could try being paid to throw the party by getting many groups together to combine their efforts or simply have fun. The **Getting You Guys Together model** has led to such services as online business-to-business exchanges, auctions, e-malls and chat environments.

The e-customer already knows what something is worth to him and technology allows complex and detailed negotiation to take place between participants anywhere in the world. This has enabled the **You Decide What Its Worth model** to flourish on auction sites, including the bidding behemoth ebay.com.

e-customer worth?"

Its close relation is the **What You Use is What You Pay model** that charges the e-customer for the exact amount of product or service that is utilized. No more buying slightly too much or too little. The e-customer loves this approach. The push to online interest rates being charged and paid daily is just one example of it in action.

It is important to change only the model not the spreadsheet. Don't fake the figures. It's not clever. And it will end in tears unless you float the company first. Which could make you a billionaire. Which is kind of clever. Unless you are fooling yourself and your investors.

The modelling business is meant to be about building sustainable money-making plans. It can end up having rather more to do with making the insubstantial look attractive by draping it over the unfeasibly beguiling.

Staying in business

Too often the business plan looks on the e-customer as a reactive consumer. In this case it makes sense to understand that simply shouting loudly (advertising) is not enough. You and your business cannot simply buy sustainable, profitable market share.

Your first worry should not be about using sufficient advertising to 'bully' your e-customer through the gates. It should be to think about the e-customer and what he wants. Just listen to a reader of *Fortune* magazine for an idea about what he is demanding:

I THINK THE BIG

He is not overly worried about your profit margin. But one of the cardinal rules of serving the e-customer is that you should still be in business to serve him at the start of each day. There is nothing reassuring about having your favourite supplier declared bankrupt.

I THINK THE **BIG QUESTION** IS,

WHO'S THINKING ABOUT THE CONSUMER?

IT DOESN'T MATTER TO ME THAT

I CAN BUY GROCERIES, FURNITURE, OR EVEN A CAR ONLINE

IF THE PROCESS DOESN'T SIMPLIFY MY LIFE.

I WANT HASSLE-FREE RETURNS,

A GOOD SELECTION, FAIR PRICES,

ON-TIME DELIVERIES, AND,

WHEN I NEED IT,

GREAT E-CUSTOMER SERVICE.

I'M CERTAINLY NOT CONCERNED WITH

PROFIT MARGINS OR THE FACT THAT THE FEDEX LOSES MONEY

EVERY TIME ONE OF ITS EMPLOYEES

STICKS A YELLOW NOTE ON MY DOOR.

INDEED, I WISH IT WAS

A LITTLE LESS FOCUSED

ON GETTING ME TO SPEND MORE PER ORDER AND

A BIT MORE ON MAKING SURE I ACTUALLY

GET WHAT I ASK FOR. [10]

At boo.com the money ran out only six months after the launch. The inside story is that poor financial management and inefficient operational controls explain where the money went. The decision, for example, to locate a call centre in the centre of the most expensive capital in the world.

Listen to the scathing comments of one critic:

FIRST IT HAD A COMIC STRIP-SOUNDING, **WACKY NAME.** IT HAD 'THE BIG IDEA', THE ONE THING THAT WOULD SET **BOO.COM** APART FROM THE REST – REVOLVING CLOTHES TO PUT PEOPLE AT EASE ABOUT SHOPPING FOR WEARABLES ONLINE.

And so now, according to some portions of the media, it's confirmed. The internet is a bubble. You really can't be a millionaire if you are under 30. And your colleagues made big mistakes when they ran away to start their own dot.com venture. That is the conclusion that some journalists have been all too happy to reach after the stock falls and the demise of certain start-up net companies.

Businesses fail all the time, its pretty common. In the US more than 14% of start-up businesses fail annually. In the UK alone there are over 21,000 failures.[11] The proportion of great schemes that have failures along the way is similarly high, and electronic business was never going to be any different.[12] Competition is a harsh master. Your investors may be even harsher. They demand returns in three years when returns in five or six would be more sensible.

It is not thinking 'This time next year we will be millionaires' that is the problem. It is the assumption that an idea is bound to be successful no matter what we do, especially in the high casualty world of retail.

But still. Don't listen too hard to those among journalists who wear their old media cynic badges proudly. They have a vested interest in delaying the spread of the new media. They also have an unhealthy jealous streak concerning all self-made riches.

The lesson here is not that the internet will have to 'put its tie back on' but that the e-customer needs to come first. That must be the big idea. Revolving clothes are only one potential ingredient in putting the big idea into place.

Boring, boring, boring

Boring, boring, boring

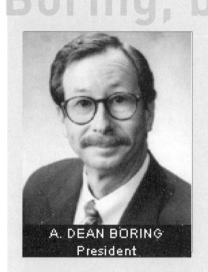

A. DEAN BORING
President

INCREDIBLE BUT TRUE. THERE REALLY IS A WEBSITE NAMED BORING.COM FOR A COMPANY CALLED BORING BUSINESS SYSTEMS. IT'S A **VERY REPUTABLE** COMPANY WITH AN ACKNOWLEDGED REPUTATION FOR QUALITY AND E-CUSTOMER SERVICE. **BUT NOT VERY INTERESTING**. THEY SAY 'BORING MEANS BUSINESS'. BUT IT DOESN'T HAVE TO.

You name it. The domain name exists somewhere with a dot.com equivalent after it. You can even play the game. Go ahead and try to guess at generic domain name addresses. From head to toe, from cradle to grave, seven days a week and 365 days a year, electronic channels are queuing up to serve each part of our bodies, minds, and schedules.

The exercise can leave you asking whether the world really needs another website. You may feel that the opportunities have all gone.

"Electronic channels

And that even the new all mobile and interactive TV channels will just mean a transfer of the existing internet material. But you would be very, very wrong. As in out of your head wrong.

The very number of such sites and channels provides a rich opportunity for **combining services.** Instead of dealing with the mess of many single benefit sites and channels the e-customer would prefer to amalgamate as many as possible – with just one password to remember and a common way of managing each.

It's one way of **making services easier** and there are so many more: improvements to the way that services are presented and used; improvements to the manner in which they are linked together; avoiding duplicated typing; creating seamless, vertical processes from searching to satisfaction.

There is also considerable potential to radically **increase interactivity** available via existing electronic channels. Many are limited to simple point and click hyperlinks. Sometimes this is spiced up visually with animated graphics but this only delivers colourful passivity. A fairly bland meal.

Part of this opportunity will be to **create deeper and richer facilities** that provide facilities and experiences that are complete: that go beyond the 'miles wide, inches deep' approach of many existing services.

These developments all combine to improve the e-customer life and avoid removing his will to live through insipid offerings. Electronic channels need to build themselves into valuable and valid enhancements to the real world. They cannot be allowed to end up as glorified business directories or mail order with pictures. They need to exploit their full potential.

need to build themselves into

valuable and valid

enhancements to the real world "

Many new e-propositions are simply not sufficiently captivating. A few examples will make the case: 'check your bank balance at 11.37 pm' (Natwest.com); 'at least you can get your email' (mail2web.com); 'shop till you drop' (btinternet.com); 'get the lowest prices' (jungle.com). If these examples seem interesting to you then be deeply concerned about your own virtual world offering. It is probably deeply coma-inducing but you are too middle of the road to notice the difference.

These examples are merely pale (or bright pink) copies of each other. It is only a matter of combining the information and technology available into services and experiences that are more attuned to the individual.

It just isn't that much more difficult (although it is still rare) to come up with something a little different that pulls in the punters. You don't need to mug[13] them. How about just building them something they just gotta try and once tried they can't live without?

Differences are the only justification for multiplicity. If we or our businesses are identical then there is no need for more than one of us. Some companies have given up their individuality for size through mergers and acquisitions. Others have simply forgotten what it means to differentiate. They do not compete. They opt merely to exist.

Companies must be individual. Their differences influence their ability to be noticed, favourably compared and chosen. Go wild. Impress the e-customer. Get rid of the same, dull, jaded, colourless offerings. Be bold! You will need better, brighter ideas, and new ways of serving the same people, or your usefulness will cease and you will become surplus to requirements.

Do something completely new

Cars allow us to drive faster, be protected from the elements, have more control. There are things that we would not even consider doing without cars. It would just take too long, be too much hassle and be too hard without them. They extend our horizons. Our possibilities. Our willingness to experiment.

In the same way, computing has made possible that which would not previously have been attempted. The human genome project has used computers to decipher the 3.1 billion bio-chemical letters of DNA. Computing power has been successfully harnessed to document the coded instructions for building and operating a fully functional human being.

It would have taken a team of 12 monks an estimated billion years to have completed the same task. And they would probably have forgotten vital information before the end of the quest. They would never have completed the task. And even if it had been finished the information would have been unusable.

In a similar way, computers can achieve for the e-customer what he has always wanted but which, in the past, it has not been feasible to deliver. That's what we should be trying to do. The move from corner shops to supermarkets occurred because they gave choice and low prices. The e-customer valued these more than personal service and home delivery. At the time it was not possible for him to have both, so he had to choose. In the future it will be possible to have both. To the advantage of e-customer and business.

The e-customer did not stop wanting it all. His pent-up demand for everything is waiting as an ally for any business that can deliver. The e-customer doesn't want to pick up his own stuff. He wants to have it all. We tend to organize shops and services to sell what the e-customer is prepared to buy. Sometimes we guess what they are willing to buy. Sometimes we copy what others are successfully selling. We then assume that is as far as the e-customer's desires, expectations and aspirations go. Then someone comes along to the market with something new and suddenly we discover that they wanted more than they had previously been getting.

Like the translucent iMac. Or the mobile phone. Or a networked computer. The portable tape recorder. Then companies copy and compete on price and features until the next innovation. The next innovation to be successful will be based around the basic needs that an e-customer just has. The problems he just has to deal with: these are irreducible, constant and potentially lucrative. My kingdom for a sword. Or my hard-earned money for …

What does he want? Just as an example, when I go to buy a product I would kind of like to know that I am making the best choice. The best set of features for the money I have. The one that is closest to my requirements.

The reason that you usually go away unsure whether that is what you have bought is that neither you nor the shop assistant can have all specifications, prices, reliability and e-customer satisfaction details of all products in your minds at any one time. But computers can have all of it in their memories available to compare.

It is not that technology cannot do the job required but that it is not being used to deliver what the e-customer wants. Saying that it is too hard will simply not do. The fact is that reasonable e-customer management systems are out there doing a pretty good job at the fundamentals. Not to have the world's most responsive system may be understandable but not to have one that meets basic requirements is certainly careless.

So if you can ensure that you are using technology to deliver what the e-customer wants you have a place on the track. A chance to compete. An opportunity to win.

It isn't (and it is) just another channel ... When

redherring.com, the technology investments magazine, advocates that e-business is 'just' business in a faster, wider medium they may be understating the truth.

The comparison holds true only in the same way as writing is just a more efficient way of repeating yourself. And in the same way as a car is just a means of travelling in a faster, easier way. Or electricity is just a log fire several times removed. Since our basic needs are the same, there are only so many categories of solution. Some of the solutions still revolutionize the way that we live our lives and work for a living.

So stop minimizing the differences. Sure, you have to look for comparisons. That's the way to understand where you are now. But don't minimize the advantages. Don't assume that the guy over at the competition isn't looking at the 'faster, wider medium', thinking about how he is going to use it to kick your butt. I would be. So would you if you understood the possibilities. Unless you really do think that technology has no repercussions in the real world.

Small advantages can lead to big wins. Genetically we share 97% of our DNA with all mammals and 99% with chimpanzees. A small difference but look at the results. Look at our relative capabilities. Look at the benefits that our differences bring in lifestyle.

It is in exploiting the differences that you will find competitive advantage. Each channel has its own characteristics that allow improvements to be made in serving the e-customer.

"It is in exploiting

Differentiation has the ability to turn previously passive e-customers into partners who actively collaborate with you in achieving mutually held objectives. Affiliation schemes enable a sharing of the wealth that is generated by working together. Joint bidding facilities allow e-customers to band together with the e-vendor to buy goods at a price and margin that suits them both.

Net technology allows such schemes to be bought off the shelf. Installation is rapid, administration largely automated, distribution instantly global. This is not possible without electronic channels. A good idea can be allowed room to grow and to grow quickly.

Net technology can make many previously uneconomical services into profitable, money-spinning winners. So reconsider stuff that your e-customers have always wanted. Ideas that would blow your competition away. Geography, manpower, turn-around times, and complexity are all diminished as obstacles to delivering exactly what the e-customer expects. Maybe even more than he expects. And how valuable could that be?

Service does not have to end at 5 pm. It does not have to be away from the desk. It can remember everything. It can work out loyalty discounts and points schemes at sub-pocket change granularity.

It allows comparison between everything and anything. Allowing you to find contrasts and trends in the behaviour of your e-customers. Powerfully supporting the e-customer in comparing goods and services from a range of providers. Best prices. Best fit features.

the differences that you will find
competitive advantage "

win

The winners become those who are the kings ...

... of the lists of search results and recommendations: at the top of them. Creating better tools for creating lists of recommended products and suppliers. Able to get to the top of the value-based, rather than price-based lists. Or even rising above the lists through greater powers of loyalty and relationship.

So now you know. It is possible to serve that e-customer better. He knows and already senses it. We have worked for a long time to meet our needs and improve our lifestyles. As a society our hunger for better lives shows no sign of abating. The internet is a key to satisfying that hunger. Get yourself a key:

- Give people more time.
- Give people better advice.
- Give people more friends.

It's good, but it's no excuse for sloppiness

The differences revealed in making the comparisons don't all come out in favour of the virtual world. Planet E is still dependent upon other channels if it is to be a complete experience.[14] Many entrepreneurs of the moment will ignore or be oblivious to this.

They will make the mistake of believing that people only want one channel. Or that they make their choices based on channel first rather than on proposition and performance.

One channel must become an extension of another. E-customers should be able to move from one location to another, back and forth effortlessly between the virtual and the real world. It should not be an either/or choice. If the web does the trick, then great; if not, then it's into the car and a trip to the mall.[15]

If the e-customer cannot find what he wants in the retail outlet because it is out of stock then he should be able to order it over the internet. And he should be able to access the net in store, on his mobile phone, at home through the TV or via the PC on his desk.

Existing businesses need to identify what has made them successful in the real world and refocus on their essential valued attributes through exploiting the available characteristics of the multiple electronic channels. This can be difficult. The further away from its founding date a business travels the harder it can be to remember why it became successful. Maybe no one in the company knows or ever knew. Faced with seismic change the 'unwritten contract of value' between corporate and e-customer is often broken without it even being remembered.

One example can be found at marksandspencers.com. After more than 100 years of ringing up profits this UK retail institution had started to believe that it was invulnerable to the remorseless pace of change. As the competition took up new positions up-market, down-market, online and off-line it simply forgot to evolve with its e-customers.

Its valued attributes of quality and the high-end shopping experience have still not been transmuted into the post-internet world. It should have said 'We are good at that but how do we move forward by using technology that allows us to do more – to give a better shopping experience?'

Too bad its virtual incarnation is so limited in scope. It doesn't allow the e-customer to find out in store what is available and when it will be delivered. There is no facility for home ordering on the internet and picking it up in the shop. Sadly it is not possible to ask for your personal shopper by name and receive advice on a purchase.

The problem is that it has not put itself in the position of its e-customers and has been unable to create products and services that they actually want. Perhaps it thinks that it is too difficult to meet the e-customers' demands.

Marks's eyes could be opened and Spencer's limited vision expanded by a review of landsend.com, a company founded in 1963 on eight enduring principles that have helped it fit right in with the possibilities of the web. Its people have grabbed hold of the enhanced abilities that the web provides because they want to serve the e-customer better.

Landsend.com has designed services based on an intuitive grasp of e-customer needs and using the help of e-customer feedback. It has got the two groups of people together to come up with some great ideas.

Together they have figured out how to allow the e-customer to 'try before she buys' by building a personal mannequin in three dimensions. This is an interactive shopping tool that helps build a wardrobe based on the e-customer's shape and lifestyle. The e-customer simply fills in her exact measurements and can then try new clothes on with a single click.

Such an idea utilizes the years of experience of their team by providing instant connections via voice or online text chat to e-customers. In this way a personal shopper can keep building the relationship by giving expert advice based on measurements and past shopping history,

Use internet-based services to your advantage

This sort of thing just can't be done as effectively without internet-based services. It exploits the abilities of the channels to the benefit of business and the e-customer. It avoids complete channel replication – doing the same old thing everywhere when each channel has distinct characteristics that should be utilized.

Such service innovations become more valuable as 'off the shelf' products become interchangeable. All those who wish to surf the growth curve of electronic channels must align themselves to networked attitudes, ethos and possibilities. If you have no net history, look back at its root to predict its future.

Amazon uses the differences well. Immense warehouses with millions of books, shared reviews between e-customers, and rapid delivery. The big portal names are successful because they do what only the internet can do. These advantages need to be explored. There aren't that many good shopping experiences on the net. This should not come as a great shock to real-world shoppers because there aren't that many good shopping experiences in real life either!

This is the opportunity. This is the threat. The internet has some inbuilt disadvantages. You do have to switch on. You do have to dial up. You do have to log in. You have to plod through it every time. The average internet download takes 22 seconds. Are people willing to wait that long? Why should they?

Of course there is even more waiting in real life but at least shopping can be considered part of real, breathing life. There is no need to wait for it to download. It can be pleasant to get out and walk around. It is more natural to most people. Irritating and time-consuming eventually, but easy to get into for most people's mindset.

This is why we see failures and slow-downs. Not enough e-businesses have answered the e-customers' burning question, 'why should I log on?' Others, including some of the stars of the third decade, may have already begun to forget or be unable to translate the historic attraction into a commercial setting.

Don't think that a new electronic service can still rely on the excitement or newness of the web. It is not a novelty. It is a fact of life. Nor can it rely on unbridled investment enthusiasm despite no profits.

So leave the ranks of the 'Rah, Rah, Dot.Coms' who cheerlead the internet movement without telling anyone what it is for. Break with tradition and avoid lecturing the e-customer without listening first. Use your marketing millions or pennies to launch advertising that asks e-customers to tell them what is wrong with shopping or banking over the net. Follow up with a set of adverts that demonstrate how your new services will overcome the problems of your competitors. Tell your e-customers that you have figured out what they hate and made it work.

Companies can turn themselves around by using the internet or another channel to compensate for their weaknesses. The idea that channels can be used to attack or defend a competitive position is not new in itself, but the speed, capacity, obviousness, possibilities and expectations are all greater. Those who get it will really get it, even if it takes a little time.

I belong to me

Freedom. Wars are fought over this precious principle. It is enshrined in constitutions and praised as the source of capitalist energy. Freedom of speech, freedom of movement, the right to say, think and believe what we want to.

The net was created to deliver interactions independent of any central controlling influence. It grew for its first 25 years on the idealism of freedom of everything. Communities grew on their own without the lure of net profits.

The e-customer is the offspring of this movement. It was never only about the science-fiction image of cyber punks sneaking into secure systems. It has been driven by the liberating power of the network to magnify the abilities of individuals to right wrongs and cure the world's ills.

The answer to the question 'Who owns the e-customer?' is that he owns himself. And the more he becomes networked the more he will seek to enjoy his rights and influence. Relationships cannot be bought, traded or owned. They can only be built between two groups who want to move beyond transactions.

Watch what happens when this truth is neglected. Try and buy your e-customers and see how little you can get for your advertising, acquisition, and loss-leading dollars. Defeating the opposition in a way that the e-customer considers unfair will only lead to a loss of trust.

"Relationships cannot be bought, traded or owned. They can only be built between two groups who want to move beyond transactions"

The original couple may stay together out of convenience or the children but it will not be the same again.

In business, as in the rest of life, it's better to make your own friends than rely on someone else to make them for you. Waiting meekly for second-hand friends may lead to a wardrobe of ill-fitting, shabby, hand-me-downs.

If you make stuff you may have decided to stay in your limited manufacturing lair. But it isn't all that smart to assume the relationship is **someone else's problem** and that all your company has to do is produce stuff for someone else to sell to the e-customer. What happens when the stuff that is required is no longer what the e-customer wants? What happens when the seller finds another product manufacturer?

If you are into **sit back and wait** retail sales then you had better hope that the manufacturers understand what the e-customer wants. You are both leaving success to chance hoping that the combination in the virtual world of some nifty graphic art and an electronic shopping cart will be enough. Even if the product and the service are both reliable and of high quality it may not be enough. You will only find that out through sales figures when they eventually filter through. Your reactive changes may not be sufficient or right for the e-customer since they are made after the problem has occurred and without consultation.

Far better to have taken the role of **relationship manager** because at least then you will have sat with the e-customer as a matter of course. Your goal is to find out what he wants and provide whatever he is buying at the moment. It is through you as a trusted supplier that the e-customer will prefer to buy.

As a product manufacturer, a decision must be made between trying to build a direct relationship with the e-customer and sharing that relationship with an intermediary of some kind. Not everything works better if it is done alone. Collaboration between many parties to support and **share the relationship** is an attractive aim but one where there is usually unequal distribution of influence.

The benefits of an integrated service

The need to have a direct relationship with the e-customer does not mean the end of amalgamating services. If all product manufacturers sold direct to their e-customers shopping could become a nightmare. Imagine having to go to separate websites for each product. The direct.com shopping list of the future might be:

- 3 apples.com

- 1 lettuce.com

- 2 loavesofbread.com

- 1 cornflakes.com

But is that so very difficult if you don't have to make the trek to the shops to make the purchases and you can choose exactly the products that you want? The web itself can be viewed as a single location shopping zone. The challenge will be in making such a system workable and desirable from the e-customer's perspective.

For a start, every item has to be delivered to the e-customer. That's OK if what you are selling is essentially electronic like software, financial services, or now music or films. It's a little trickier when you need to transport it physically to the e-customer's door. It's even more difficult when the separate items on the shopping list need to arrive at the same time.

Who makes sure that the deliveries are made together to reduce costs and increase convenience to the e-customer? Is that a supermarket or a department store or a retailer in a different guise? Does the company that makes the deliveries also offer shopping list management software and how does that differ from any retailer.com at the moment?

The key difference should really be where the relationship sits. Any sensible manufacturer would work towards a position where they have the benefits of a direct relationship along with the benefits of an integrated service. So perhaps a range of direct brands could get together to set up an integrated service that has the clear objective of integrating ordering and delivering while allowing brands to be distinctively sold and providing them with their own set of e-customer behaviour data and analysis.

Does that sound like a mall or a shopping centre? Shared amenities, individual brands and experiences. You're right, but some e-malls attempt to exert far more control over the relationship than is healthy for the product manufacturer and still leave too much of the infrastructure around the e-customer to the manufacturer or retailer to provide.

The networked basis of electronic channels will continually allow the e-customer to leave one provider for another. It is always possible for a new amalgamating layer to be placed above the current relationship holder. Or for someone lower down the relationship chain to reach up and deal with the e-customer direct.

Consider the experience of a traditional farm in the UK where the Counsell family have lived and worked the land for 600 years. In 1999, they launched their own website, somersetorganics.com, to rapturous applause from their (international) e-customers:

I WILL NEVER AGAIN

BUY CONVENTIONAL MEAT.

WHAT A DIFFERENCE THERE IS BETWEEN THIS AND ORGANIC MEAT!

I'VE EATEN ORGANIC MEAT FOR SOME THREE MONTHS NOW

AND THE TASTE IS OUT OF THIS WORLD.

I'M SURE I CAN TASTE THE HERBS THAT

THE ANIMALS GRAZE ON AND THE TEXTURE IS FANTASTIC.

WELL DONE SOMERSET LEVELS ORGANIC FOODS!

> **"The networked basis of electronic channels will continually allow the e-customer to leave one provider for another"**

If Mr Counsell and his son Richard can swap a cow for a computer (true story!) invest £5,000 and find their very own golden goose (or should that be beef?) then so can anyone who wants to really deliver what their e-customers want. The sophistication and friendliness of the site outstrips many of the efforts of the more sizeable opposition.

The e-customer will choose to establish and build relationships with whomever he wishes. Interconnectivity will allow his true preferences to be realized. He may always have wanted to avoid the middle man or have someone to take care of all his individual purchases. The decision is his.

The

e-customer

... and also your difficult customers: they are probably the same people 99

Will the real e-customer please stand up? So who is
the e-customer? How will the world that he inhabits impact on our society, its structure and culture, and how should business reorganize and re-group to meet and exploit these changes?

The business world stereotypes the e-customer at its peril. The e-customer is not who you think he is. The distinction between hyped, shoddy research presented as fact and the truth is dramatic. The lack of understanding in traditional business, government and consultancies is often profound. They just don't get it.

" The e-customer does not care

The e-customer does not care about traditional boundaries between products, organizations or departments. The e-customer wants an improved lifestyle and will remain loyal to the source of simplicity, care and good value. The available propositions to the e-customer are therefore simple but not necessarily straightforward.

Eventually everybody will use the net in equal portions if they can afford to do so. It's so obvious that it hardly needs statistical proof. Every month a new story appears in the old media proclaiming that first women, then the old, and then the young are the fastest growing internet users.

As an example, 20% of the net users in the US are 42–50 year olds which means that they are growing faster than the 18–24 year olds. There is a simple explanation. There is a greater proportion of the 18–24 market on the net already. That's why the growth has slowed. The message has taken longer to get into the minds of the older users and is now shooting through the high growth groups.

Demographics are barely useful when trying to understand who the e-customer has become. He is not the same person that his post code or income grouping suggest. In buying the electronic dream, the e-customer has opened up his mind to more than the ability to buy his cat's flea collars at pets.com without moving from his chair.

Now this may not be the fault of those who do not understand. It is a natural consequence of what is often a total lack of experience and exposure to the inner workings of the e-world. When I meet with

traditional boundaries
between products, organizations or
departments 99

business leaders I often ask a few straightforward questions to gauge
their level of practical comprehension. Simply put, I enquire how
many of the many available e-experiences they have had.

There are different reasons for e-blindness. Sometimes it is
generational. Those who didn't grow up with the new technology and
concepts will often use them but with a limited grasp of their potential.
Sometimes it is attitudinal. Those who do not want to hear because
they reject change and minimize the advantages of anything that they
do not understand.

E-vision is created at the point where knowledge of the multiple
electronic channels is combined with the mind transplant necessary
for empathy with the e-customer. Electronic channels bring with them
networked attitudes and these are not immediately understood by
those who attempt to set up shop.

Anarchic e-customer
Just for starters bear in mind that the net has anarchic tendencies. This
is vital information whether you are on the 'net offence' going out to
defeat corporate Goliaths or on the 'net defence' trying hard to avoid
ever more dangerous Davidic start-ups.

Woah! you could say. Anarchy. Sounds risky. Better not do that. We
need rules.

Consider the fundamentals of anarchy. It believes in 'rational'
authority. It believes in 'right' before 'might'. It claims that those in

authority should be there because they are 'authorities'. That those in charge should be experts at helping, supporting and leading their charges to better, greater things.

RATIONAL AUTHORITY

IS BASED ON COMPETENCE

AND IT HELPS THE PERSON WHO LEANS ON IT TO GROW.

IRRATIONAL AUTHORITY

IS BASED ON POWER
AND SERVES TO EXPLOIT

THE PERSON SUBJECTED TO IT.[16]

The internet has this kind of impact because it removes many of the benefits of being institutionalized. Of being established. Of being Big. Most people shop at the biggest, nearest supermarket. Therefore the supermarket that can have the most stores should in principle have the advantage. It is hard for entrants to have as many stores because it costs so much to build them.

This is a very good thing for the big supermarket. But not so great for the customer.

With the internet these advantages are diminished. The sites are all equidistant. No key advantages are to be gained by grabbing land in prime locations. The closest things to the land grab approach are the 'domain name registration' frenzy and the 'partnering' rush. Even here the internet offers a humble alternative: the search engine.

Type in what you want and you don't always get the biggest and the richest. The establishment may attempt to influence the outcomes but so can the new kids. Some search engines can be paid, quite properly, to influence outcomes (go.com, msn.com) but even here the fees paid are per successful result, giving an equal opportunity to anyone who can turn those searches into sales.

Proximity in distance is being replaced by proximity to the heart. Favourites. A creation of the web generation. Just create your own library, university or shopping mall. Pull it down from a menu. And there you are surrounded by old friends. Type in what you are looking for and you may find better, new friends just as quickly.

Of course there is still huge advantage to being well known. And well known can be connected to an ability to afford huge advertising budgets. However, the popular and the useful can outperform the large and the powerful.

Omniscient e-customer

Do you still think that you can keep your dirty laundry between you and the washer? Are you sure that the next corporate scandal will not come from within? Or that poor e-customer experiences will remain small-time news? Or that critical analyst or governmental reports will stay under wraps?

Consider the experience of a restaurant in New York, listed in Michelin and famed as a food establishment of finesse and quality. Unfortunately when the New York Sanitary Department came to call they also decided to publish the results of their inspection of this and other restaurants on the net.

The report from New York City Public Health Sanitarians mentions vermin in the air. The outraged proprietor complained that he did not consider 'a single fly' as tantamount to vermin. He has hopefully learned the 'no more secrets' rule.

Private information on the web just has a habit of appearing. Whether it's the contents of sensitive Microsoft documents (opensource.com) or rumours relating to Monica Lewinsky. It's the combination of low distribution costs, ease of manipulating multiple sources of data, and the possibility of publishing anonymously.

When Suharto ruled Indonesia, he used a 50,000-strong Department of Information to muzzle the press. That department no longer exists. But it illustrates the difficulty of restraining the flow of information. And where it cannot be stopped it is best to focus on simply utilizing the natural flows for the advantage of the business.

For an example of this in action, try 192.com. This is a UK site that combines telephone directory information, lists of those eligible to vote, and other available information. If you are a star with democratic ideals you will find your address published, despite your deep desire for privacy.

Of course the e-customer does not know everything but perhaps it is better to assume that he does. It is probable that anything really sensitive or really valuable will eventually reach him. It is foolish in the extreme to believe either that secrets will remain secrets or that your e-customer will come to you uninformed.

The e-customer will become the expert in areas that affect him. He is naturally often more motivated in meeting his own needs than those of the businesses that are serving him. His life is impacted by what he buys and does. Increasingly he will arrive with you informed and ready to compare.

" Private information on the web just has a habit of appearing "

Ever-changing e-customer

A problem with the e-customer is that he doesn't live in a vacuum. Each and every moment of the day there are new experiences, tastes, fashions. No particular offering or brand will remain immune to these changes if it does not adapt with the e-customer.

Electronic life encourages curiosity and heightens impatience. Attention spans diminish for particular sources of information, entertainment and purchases. Think pop music. Think fashion. It's not that a recording artist stops creating decent music but that the audience has grown up or grown tired. They throw themselves at the next big thing.

Businesses have treated the e-customer as interchangeable, and so he has become. If the relationship is reduced to transactions it will be unable to maintain influence when the e-customer is becoming restless. One day soon the difference between providers will become as indistinguishable to e-customers as e-customers have become to their providers.

How to cope? The business must become as curious and impatient for change as its e-customers. It must creatively destroy and reinvent, while maintaining common threads that ensure continuity and develop loyalty.

Look at fashionable icons that endure. They manage to do so by collaboration and association. By continually spending time seeking inspiration that will enable them to come out ahead of the progress of their audience.

Consider Tom Jones, who 35 years after achieving his first hit record did so again in 2000. In a move of genius, he combined his enduring strengths of mighty vocals and room-filling physical energy with the credibility and fashionable musical sensitivities of a different artist on every track of his new triple-platinum-selling album. The result, *Reload*, has now sold over 2 million copies and has enabled him to be introduced to the fan bases of each of the artists involved in each track.

Influential e-customer

It would be comforting to think that the opinions of this demanding individual could be ignored. To assume somehow that the opinions of surfers are less important than those of the rest of the world. It's tempting to align thinking with that sardonic American icon, little Bart Simpson:

MILHOUSE WE **NEED TO TELL EVERYONE** – LET'S GET THIS STORY ON TO THE INTERNET.

BART **NO** – WE NEED TO GET THIS TO PEOPLE **WHOSE OPINIONS REALLY MATTER.**[17]

This compares starkly with the invitation issued by *Vanity Fair*, self-proclaimed magazine for the rich, to the e-customer:

ARE YOU AN OPINION LEADER? **DO YOU** INFLUENCE YOUR FRIENDS AND FAMILY? **ARE YOU** ON THE CUTTING EDGE OF NEW PRODUCTS AND SERVICES, WORLD AND CULTURAL EVENTS? **IF YOU** ANSWERED 'YES' TO ANY OF THESE QUESTIONS, THEN VANITY FAIR INVITES **YOU** TO BECOME **A MEMBER** OF THE CHATTER, VANITY FAIR'S ONLINE **OPINION** LEADER GROUP.

Whether business strategy is safe in agreeing with the 'Bartster' is questionable. It will certainly make the e-customer laugh but he's unlikely to pay to enjoy the joke. The opinions and interests of those using electronic channels are essential to the long-term success of any business.

It is essential to get in among e-customer and not merely attempt to discover them through management reports or the statistics. It is in immersing the business in the renewing waters of the internet that it can be reborn. It becomes possible to ride the wave to the next destination of cultural and technological discovery.

Knowing the opinions of your e-customers is important if you wish to influence them, and those that they influence, and in turn, look through them into the future of the world, society and commerce. It is vital to find better ways of connecting with them, involving them, and using their vitality to educate your own offer and its delivery.

Star Trek expectations

We are going to live in a society where you can order a new body part. If we can do this then surely someone should be able to work out what time my dishwasher repair man will arrive. You would think so, wouldn't you?

The marketing frenzy, media interest and science-fiction depictions of the benefits of advanced technology have set the expectations of the e-customer. When the e-customer approaches the shiny, new world of interactive service he expects to experience what he has seen in so many science-fiction visions from Star Trek to the Jetsons. Consider the sentiments of one e-customer:

WE SHOULD HAVE **CONVEYOR BELTS** IN OUR HOUSES ...

WE SHOULD BE ABLE TO JUST PRESS A BUTTON,

AND BOOKAH!! STUFF IS DONE FOR US.

I WONDER IF WE WILL EVER LIVE

LIKE THE JETSONS.

Far from being dismissed as nonsense, such visions are informing much of the research conducted by our technology companies: flexible electronic newspapers; home appliances that can talk to each other, to the e-customer, and to his grocery store.

Imagine this kind of scenario:

HE IS **REMINDED** THAT IT IS HIS WIFE'S ANNIVERSARY THE NEXT DAY. HE CHECKS HIS WIFE'S ANNIVERSARY WISH LIST AND **FINDS** HOME-COOKED CHINESE FOOD NEAR THE TOP. **HE ASKS** FOR THE INGREDIENTS FOR A LOW-FAT, CHINESE MEAL TO BE AVAILABLE AT HOME IN TWO DAYS TIME. THE REFRIGERATOR CHECKS ITS CONTENTS AND SCANS THE STORE CUPBOARD BEFORE ORDERING UP THE MISSING ITEMS FROM THE **BEST VALUE PROVIDERS** AND PASSING ON THE COOKING INSTRUCTIONS TO THE MICROWAVE AND ITS '**HOW TO COOK' DISPLAY PANEL.**

The technologies required to deliver this vision already exist. Computing power in the home will continue to increase through direct PC purchases and the integration of computers into everyday appliances. This will provide the infrastructure to build services that move towards meeting the e-customer expectations.

The business services and applications required to support such an infrastructure are appearing. They have not delivered the whole, but the components are being made to work. As the fictional becomes feasible it will move rapidly towards being the essential. Some will eagerly grab hold of such possibilities and create services that are so appreciated by the e-customer that he will abandon those who have not made the same level of effort on his behalf.

The technology is sometimes criticized for being irksome, unwieldy, obtrusive and unhelpful, but it is only a tool-set. The challenge is with the experienced creators who can plug in and combine the components to the net advantage of the e-customer. It is the service providers who will create the value and keep moving the economy along.

The e-customer wants the vision but he cannot have his dream without help and he would prefer to do as little work as possible to achieve it. Any effort expended on his part has to be taken away from the subconcious calculation that he performs when considering whether the effort is worth the payback.

When put to the test, mobile phones and cars have passed. What can you do with powerful new integrating technologies (XML) that will allow systems to talk to systems without elapsed years of re-work? What will it take to move the e-customer to the same unerring conclusion about wireless networking, talking appliances, personalized content or fibre optic glasses?

We can see why Tom Cruise wears his e-shades in the film *MI-2*. They're cool. They are wirelessly linked via satellites back to all the mission data he needs to accomplish the impossible. He would never leave on an assignment without them. If you can position technology to create similar acceptance of benefit with the e-customer then you will become indispensable. Part of the dream. And that's a very good place to be.

E-volving customer

The e-customer is an enhanced, magnified version of everything that homo consumer has always wanted to be. The efforts of one section to improve, innovate and get rich are feeding an insatiable desire from a wider section of mankind to expect more.

We all want life to get better, so once we have finished with the basic details of getting fed and being warm our attention turns to fashion, comfort, entertainment and fulfilment. These are promised to us by the adverts (if they are any good) and bit by bit our systems for delivering those promises seem closer to the ideal.

This will be a bit of a culture shock for those groups used to delivering mediocre or poor service. Suddenly it is possible for the ideas and high service standards of a small group of people to be replicated and offered to e-customers infinitely. When services are delivered electronically there is a reduced need for training and procedures manuals that attempt to transfer best practice theory into a great e-customer experience.

The level of service delivered electronically is more likely to remain consistent on future occasions. Bad and good service when automated can be repeated infinitely. This notion tends to stick in the mind of the e-customer who does not give the service the benefit of the doubt in the way he would to human provision.

“ Everyone **gets annoyed**

but the e-customer

Reluctant e-customer

It is rare to find a neutral e-customer even among those who do not use the internet. People experience guilt that they don't use it or resentment that they have to feel guilty. Talk to those who don't use it and there are often strong reactions. Reasons are given for not using it. Some are quite defensive. They say it's a load of rubbish. Or that they are old-fashioned. The more sophisticated they are the more detailed their reasoning for not using it.

For example, my doctor's excuse is that he does not want to waste his whole life browsing the internet. He wants to get to the meat of things and is not ready to open up his life to the demands of e-mail. The real problem becomes clear when he also admits that his team have almost no computer skills.

Service saboteur
Everyone gets annoyed once in a while but the e-customer gets mad more often. He gets even more effectively and he is more vocal than ever. To illustrate this take a look at a range of complaints pulled from lividchicken.com. This is a site dedicated to 'all things that get you annoyed', complete with sections about home annoyances to road rage:

nce in a while
gets mad
more often"

- Spam (not the chopped pork and ham variety).

- Free ISP CD-ROMs – they make effective frisbees I hear.

- Search engines that either list zero results or a million results.

- Websites that take ages to download.

- When you're looking for a website and the error message comes up.

- Chain e-mails.

- Adverts and pop-up banners on websites.

What they reveal is that there is plenty that annoys the e-customer. More importantly that many of the beloved weapons available to the e-marketers are not that popular. The e-customer doesn't like a diet of spam, free CD-ROMS, chain e-mails or pop-up banners. And yet that is often what we feed him.

He's going to spew it out or seek to change his diet. Don't assume that he loves the benefits of the e-world so much that he will put up with irritations. He will go where there are fewer of them or become negatively motivated by seeing your company name associated with them. And when that happens the estimated $300 a head your competitors spend to attract the e-customer is buying them worse than zero benefit.

But back to the disagreeable Mr, Mrs, Ms or Miss E. If you wind him up he's going to want to get even. And there are so many ways of doing it.

Let's play Jekyll and Hyde

So why is it that our e-customer has a Dr Jekyll transformation as soon as he starts to interact over electronic channels? Instead of showing patient understanding, he displays zero tolerance for delays and mistakes.

Evidence suggests that the change to 'Bad-Ass Consumer' can be attributed to something perfectly understandable going on between his brain (the thinking bit), his subconscious (the 'where did that come from?' thinking bit), the means of communication (the screen and the internet) and the information he has received about computers in general and the internet in particular.

Let's look at the **means of communication** and its attributes. (*Q*. What do you call a gorilla using the internet? *A*. Anything you like – he can't reach you.) It stands to reason that separating consumers physically from those that serve them will make them a little less intimidated. Since you can be anyone over the internet it makes sense to choose to be a bold, demanding consumer rather than a doormat.

Another attribute of the net that encourages consumer action is of course that it provides a global audience for (even) your (bizarre) views with a minimum of effort and expense. A quick look at the (mainly American) phenomenon of anti-business websites supports this view. Just consider the following:

- walmartsucks.com

- disneysucks.com

- skysucks.com

Set up by irate consumers keen to make their (alleged) corporate tormentors pay dearly for their (alleged) dastardly deeds, these sites are both impressively popular and effective.

Often less impressive is the way that some target companies have responded. They should have recognized the need that these sites meet and provided similar feedback mechanisms on their official sites. They should have encouraged opinions and suggestions. It is better to know about an issue before it escalates into bad publicity, an unhappy e-customer, or legal action.

Instead many companies have tried to shut down the 'anti' websites through legal action. Others ignore them. Some do not seem to know that they exist. While others pour over their details in an effort to find wrongdoing.

Hiding the complaints department telephone numbers and e-mail addresses just does not work to the commercial advantage of a company. The e-customer still has the complaint and the complaint will remain unresolved. And worse, he is telling the world about it!

On average without e-mail he will tell seven other people. With e-mail, it will become everyone on his e-mailing list. It's easy to take the effort to forward an electronic warning to the world – it's viral marketing gone bad. The facility for messages of interest to spread quickly from group to group will happen for bad news *and* good news. Which do you think will happen quickest?

Why treat the e-customer as the enemy? It seems infantile and insulting to avoid the issues that they may have. It's like hiding behind the counter until the e-customer leaves the shop. And letting the e-customer leave the shop or the website without figuring out why they are unhappy is super bad business.

And then you have the **information** that is given to the e-customer about the internet. To believe the advertising, the internet solves everything and all problems instantly. No hitches, glitches or waiting. Every billboard, every advertisement, everywhere promising the delighted consumer. Even when normal companies have a web address they suggest that service and prices and the whole dang experience will be 21st century. And all you get is a hard to navigate, mediocre playback of the company you recognize from the high street.

Let's look at some examples of internet headlines and advertising. A quick comparison with reality usually does the job of breeding e-customer dissatisfaction:

- 'Buy from them and pay more or buy.com and pay less' (buy.com).

- 'To make sure you're better off open the box below' (first-e.com).

- 'It lets you do whatever you want, wherever you are – online' (siemens.de).

- 'The world at your fingertips' (orange.co.uk).

- 'Be free to save money and time' (freeserve.com).

- 'Define your own universe' (lineone.net).

- 'Dreams made real' (agilent.com).

Of course some net based services do deliver what they promise. That's good for them but it raises expectations yet further. When the e-customer then hits an underperformer it is clear almost immediately. He will recognize the differences, make the comparison and ask himself why one service is so much better than the other.

The area of service process is becoming a key battleground for e-customers. For the first time some companies are patenting processes for serving e-customers. This leaves competitors faced with a choice of either ceasing to use a process, paying to use it, or finding and patenting a new method that is as good or better than the existing one. Deciding what can and cannot be patented may give everyone with e-customers cause for worry.

E-customers will not appreciate those who prevent improvements in the system but they will still keep buying if similar improvements are not available elsewhere. It would be wise to consider what innovations you have that could be similarly protected. If you have nothing original

"The area of service process is becoming **a key battleground** for e-customers"

enough to protect in the ideas box then be concerned. You need to match breakthrough against breakthrough to be seen as the e-customer's natural ally.

The watchdog movement

If you choose not to involve your e-customer positively in the business then do not think that he will return to passivity. The frustrated e-customer will still find a release for his unwanted creativity, especially when you not being interested led to him being poorly served.

Internationally, e-customers are becoming less, not more, satisfied: a 6% drop in overall e-customer satisfaction according to Purdue University in the last year. At the same time they are becoming more militant. They have not been slow to realize the power of the new media for airing their views and getting results.

Try this for example. Thwarted by corporate indifference, a group of Wal-Mart employees set up a site dedicated to all that is bad about the world's biggest retailer. The result, Walmartsucks.com.

It was unveiled to significant interest from many more e-customers who collectively called themselves the Wal-Mart Victims. The site includes a bulletin board, e-mail newsletter, news from the Mart and a catalogue of the sins (real, alleged, or imaginary) that have been committed against its e-customers and employees. Cranks? It has received 416,000 visitors over the past 24 months. Frustration levels are often the only difference between a crank and an e-customer.

Or how about Skysucks.com. A similar (although less ambitious) site from a man who promises to take you into the (allegedly) murky world of Sky Television.

Loving the unlovable

You say to me that it's all very well talking about this lovey, dovey, namby, pamby, wishy, washy, yes sir, no sir. Nano this, Nano that world where we love our e-customers. But they ain't that lovable in the real world.

They want more than they want to give. They want it cheaper than we can provide it. They don't know when to stop asking. Our job is to fool them into thinking that they are getting a bargain before they end up running our business into the ground.

Sometimes they make you want to spit. There are good e-customers and there are bad e-customers. And lots in between the extremes. You need to make some choices. Not a simplistic 'are they rich?'. But rather a way of doing business that encourages the good while discouraging the bad.

You need to convince the e-customer that you are a service they want to keep around. Rather like a reliable gardener. You don't want to lose him. Good ones are hard to find. This is how the best actors and doctors work. They are so in demand that the nature of the relationship can be refined and improved. Because both sides want to work together.

Service rage, the stuff that makes the e-customer see red, cannot simply be ignored. Such incidents need to be explicitly, deliberately and positively used to build relationships and improve the service for every e-customer that follows.

Someone will just have to figure out what they really want and what has made them lose their cool. Their unreasonable demands can be channelled into competitive advantages – providing difficult stuff that your e-customers want before the competition even knows it is an issue. The e-customer is not always right but you can make things work by preparing for the interaction. By planning for the confrontation.

When your e-customer is not being very smart you may screw up your face, frown, or sigh despairingly. The trick is not just to be smug in your superiority. You need to judge your service by how it is accessible for the 'not smart in the same way as you are' people.

If you reject them you limit yourself to a potential group of satisfied e-customers that only includes people like you. And who says that smart people are ever satisfied? Perhaps the dissatisfied e-customer knows something you don't.

Electronic channels have a powerful set of capabilities that should make businesses want to spend more time with their e-customers. It should free you up to provide preposterously better service. Service that will gain a reputation and scare away the competition.

The e-customer will judge your efforts to determine how sincere they really are. Don't allow yourself to offer only the rhetoric of feedback. Invitations to the e-customer to give you ideas for improvements or to share complaints are not meant to be textual padding. Such initiatives increase expectations and so demand serious, rigorous management.

Fan clubs and user communities

The networked nature of electronic channels invites the creation of e-customer communities. Connections between people. Shared meetings. Threads of thinking. Common bulletin boards. Private/public jokes. Secrets. These have existed on the net since it was first taken out of the box in the 1960s.

Government scientists and academics used what was known as ARPANET[18] to share findings and anecdotes. The famous New York based well.org created trading communities and discussion groups. The world wide web of connected documents joined together with hyperlinks was envisaged to glue together people and their thinking to create a larger, better whole.[19]

It is this legacy that you need to use to get closer to the e-customer. You need to blur the boundaries of business by providing valuable services without receiving direct payment. Such services are not expensive or difficult to establish but they give the e-customer a stake in what you are doing. You become his agent. Part of the same team. And that can become very powerful.

Pharmaceutical giant Ares-serono took this route when it established a multiple sclerosis website to allow e-customers to discuss and promote their cause. Specifically this was to gain better treatment for them or their family members. Since Ares-serono is a manufacturer of a treatment that promises to ameliorate the condition it has much to gain from the success of e-customer pressure groups.

New graffiti-based services like those offered by tourbar.com and utok.com add an extra layer to the electronic browsing experience. They allow any registered e-customer to add notes to any website. They might talk about what they liked and disliked about various sites or alternative sites for the same services that do a better job.

Rather like the ghosts in the Bruce Willis film *Sixth Sense*, the opinions of other e-customers float around after they have departed to dispense wisdom and issue warnings. Already some are criticizing such schemes for littering up the web, but since you can only see them if you choose to, the argument is not convincing.

graffiti

It suggests that the idea of e-customers gathering together and sharing information is worrying to certain rigid mindsets. Critics wish to 'defend' the battlements of fortress 'business'. But from whom? Invading hoards of e-customers armed with credit cards? No defence is necessary. These guys are the guests and allies. If they have something to say then you might as well learn from it.

❝Ever wanted

Far better to start reading the comments yourselves! Ever wanted to know what was in the mind of the e-customer? This is your chance. All too easy to position guides at the front of your site to welcome in the guests, read their graffiti and deal with their concerns. All you need to do is register for the schemes and hang out. Maybe even float along in this other dimension to competitors' sites looking for inspiration.

While you are opening up your mind you should add a variety of other communications facilities. Functionally this means your own text chat to allow real-time conversation from the first occasion when an e-customer visits the channel or site. It should also include video phones and voice chat.

But becoming an integral part of a community is about playing a role that is needed in that community: or inviting in e-customers to play a vital role in your work. You can set up e-customer advisory boards that assess products and services – asking your own fan base what you need to do to improve.

One hundred thousand screaming fans

Run 'e-customer of the month' awards to find the greatest enthusiasts for your company. This is motivating to your team. Valuable information is reaped about what enthuses people about the product. Ideas for selling the benefits to the, as yet, unconverted are also discovered.

A company that becomes an extension of the social group – that says something specific about its e-customers – is more likely to win loyalty

to know

what was in the mind of the e-customer? "

and deal with hard times. All parties will learn together what really distinguishes their group from the competition.

Once you have such a set of enthusiasts on board you will be able to benefit from user testing with passion. You will be able to adopt the practices of software companies.

Companies used to release products as finished and then had to deal with the problems that only a wider user community can uncover. This led to frustration for the users and costly re-issues for the company. Now they have turned the early releases into an advantage for them and the e-customer. They simply release alpha (very early) and beta (soon to be released) versions of the software into the user community.

It turns the whole problem around. You can go further and approach the ideal of the 'open source' movement.

Instead of dealing with complaints about bugs in the system, companies are delivering a hot, new toy to expert users who are more than happy to let them know about the faults and help fix them. The enthusiast feels more involved the process. His software is then released with his ideas and features. That's ownership. The wider, non-enthusiast community is then able to enjoy a service with fewer bugs and better features.

The very best e-services treat the e-customer as a grown-up part of solving the problem. They adopt a co-operative stance that allows them to experiment in full view of the die-hard fans.

The fan club should receive news before everyone else. They should be given passwords into unreleased parts of the service. They should be asked to edit content and improve the way it is structured.

The product needs to mean something in the real world and in the real psyche of the e-customer. That is the true nature of e-customer loyalty. A bond that endures even when the company messes up. Belief that carries e-customers with you in hard times. You stick by them and they will stick by you.

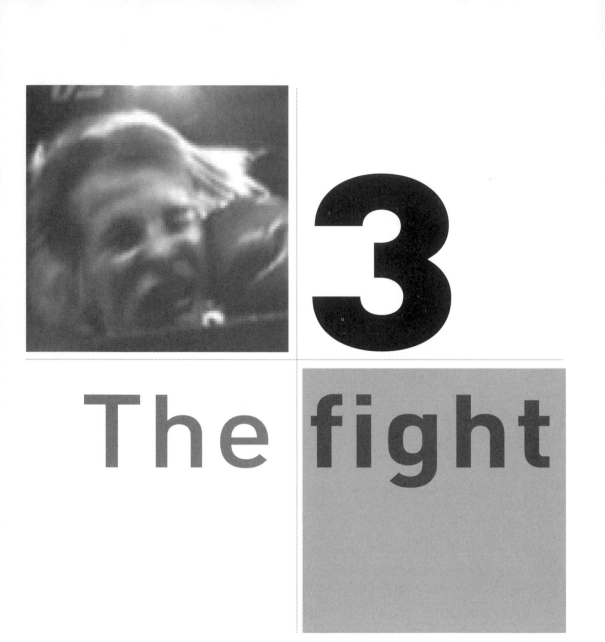

3

The fight

The challenge

Through the looking glass

The internet is another place, not necessarily a different dimension but a different country. There is stuff that the e-customer will recognize, once he has figured it out and determined that there is nothing scary here.

A significant challenge for the 'real worlders' coming into the e-world is figuring out what has happened to the familiar functions, locations and processes. They are all here but somehow they have been warped, transmuted into something 'other worldly'.

Faced with their own relative ignorance, some business people offer some standard responses. They talk loudly about the net being 'only another channel' by which they usually infer that the internet is only a form of TV broadcast over telephone wires. They are of course right about ' the other channel' bit but wrong to assume that a simplistic grasp of it will be sufficient to create competitive advantage.

It is more useful and accurate to describe the internet as a 'parallel universe'. A little like the fantasy worlds of Lewis Carroll, George Lucas, J.K. Rowling or the Wachowski brothers, it provides a mirrored world where many of the familiar objects of the real world are present but distorted, warped, transformed or enhanced. Symbolism is rife and 'not everything is what it seems'.

In the real world, we expect wisdom to be dispensed by government, agony aunts, serious-suited financial advisers, and religious leaders. In the fantasy worlds just mentioned, we may find wisdom coming from wizards, caterpillars, cookie-dispensing oracles, or a wizened, green creature with pointed ears.

" In the net world, the e-customer may also turn to

unexpected sources

In the net world, the e-customer may also turn to unexpected sources for help, advice and recommendations. What may appear to be a shop turns out to be a library and what looks like a weird hobby turns out to be a serious political mechanism.

Can you help the e-customer? Have you any idea where you are when he asks for directions? Have you made all the preparations for him? What kind of a host are you going to be?

And how about your responsibilities towards your team, your people, those that you lead? They can be as lost as even the most novice e-customer. And under more pressure because they have to get some work done in this alien environment.

Many e-customers come to the net because they want to and they have an enthusiasm for the medium. Many corporate teams come to the net because they feel forced to by the actions of competitors or the desires of shareholders. They may end up holding the reins of a new e-project without having bought anything over the internet, without experiencing online chat, setting up their own home pages, or any of the other standard internet activities.

Of course any novice is going to feel less than comfortable in his new-found virtual surroundings. He is suddenly focusing on a world made up of electronic forms, buttons, mouse clicks, and digital pictures – like living somewhere in between a pile of brochures and the insides of a TV set.

Many e-customers log in for less than positive reasons. Fear of being behind the times. He may be here because he needs to save money. Or save his job. Or help his children with their homework assignments. Not because he loves this brave new cyber concoction.

for help, and advice
and recommendations "

Either way it is your responsibility as host and guide to make him feel comfortable. To sit him down. Offer him a drink. Plump up those cushions. Remember his name and act interested in what he is saying. Make the introductions and ensure that he gets what he came for.

The experienced traveller is often dismissive of the new, lost, flustered, lobster-red holidaymaker. But the travel industry cannot afford to service only the experienced traveller. It needs the expert and the novice. And it needs to turn the 'dip your toe' travel newbies into the hardened, experienced travellers of the future. This is market development. This is e-customer development. 'We are friends', you say to the e-customer. 'Let's figure this one out together.'

The e-customer may have a lot more experience than the corporate team that is trying to sell to him. Where the experience is unequal, businesses are placed at a disadvantage. It can limit their empathy for the perspective of the e-customer. It can prevent them from creating products, services, marketing, and processes that exploit the characteristics and possibilities of the net.

Managers find it hard enough to understand the e-customer's perspective even without electronic channels involved. Recognizing this challenge, Harvard Business School run a course on customer behaviour with Professor Gerald Zaltman telling students:

UNDERSTANDING THE E-CUSTOMER IS AT THE HEART OF BUSINESS STRATEGY. CUSTOMERS **ARE VERY DIVERSE.** SIMILARLY, MANAGERS MAY RESPOND DIFFERENTLY TO THE SAME CUSTOMER DATA. **MARKET DYNAMICS** ARE THE JOINT PRODUCTS OF CUSTOMERS AND MANAGERS, THE INTERSECTIONS OF E-CUSTOMER AND MANAGER THINKING.

EXERCISING **YOUR IMAGINATION** AND TAKING RISKS AS YOU INTERPRET CUSTOMER DATA AND DEVELOP **ACTION PLANS** REQUIRES **DISCIPLINED THINKING,** HAVING THE COURAGE OF YOUR CONVICTIONS, CAREFUL CONSIDERATION OF AVAILABLE AND **DESIRED** EVIDENCE, A TOLERANCE FOR DISCOMFORT,

AND ABOVE ALL FUN.

The only way of getting your team into the position where they can act as guides will be to allow them to 'take those risks' and to introduce them to the virtual world in its full depth. They will need acclimatization. They must be capable of thinking ahead of the e-customer to anticipate his needs. This is not possible if they are running behind trying to keep up.

Someone in your company needs to chart the internet. They need to make it navigable which will require comparison with real-world objects, places, and more familiar experiences. And so first they will need to understand it for themselves.

Go to the people

If some people won't come to the internet, the internet will simply have to go to them. They still have problems that need to be solved. There is still money to be made in solving them. And it will be easier and more profitable in the short and long term to solve those problems with the power of the net.

Technologies become more human as humans become more technological – as technology becomes just part of the scenery. The initially startling technology of the telephone has become less and less shocking as it has become more advanced. The television has turned into a friendly voice in the background for many people.

Eventually the big technology 'teddy bear' is going to reach its loving arms around the whole world. It will reach down to the least willing or able and make electronic channels work for them.

We need an internet for the person who doesn't know what an espresso is. Don't even talk to him about Boolean. Just as the text-dominated world of DOS and UNIX allowed only the technophile in, so the point-and-click environment will still not be sufficiently friendly for some.

"Networked information and people are a must"

We are looking at services for people who cannot plan and cannot wait. That means the mobile internet. It means the kiosk internet. It means the invisible internet. It means the delivered to the e-customer via a real person internet. Networked information and people are a must. Any e-customer will have similarly high expectations of low prices and high value even if they do not want to use the net in its naked (or semi-clothed) form.

The boring stuff will keep getting cheaper (less profitable) while interesting stuff will keep its prices high and climbing. It will always be possible for the supply of easily copiable, dull, and uninspired stuff to exceed demand. Interesting, cool and value-rich stuff is just not so easy to copy and the e-customer will literally not be able to get enough of it. That's a recipe for a high margin, low cost, e-customer success story.

Interactive television

Create 'to die for' stuff for the e-customer who watches karaoke challenge and for those who take part in it. For the stylish and unstylish. Bring it to the 50% who may buy a computer or interactive TV but certainly don't know how it works.

Combining TV and commerce – an ideal mixture. Think of the angles, choices and statistics already available to the viewers of interactive sport. Using similar concepts it will be possible to link a TV show naturally into a one-stop shop for counselling, projects and sales surrounding the key theme. Interactive TV is an ideal e-customer service but only when it is expanded and opened up to innovation and community.

Just imagine the tie-ins between channels and selling stuff. You know a lot about the person that is watching, and even more if you can learn what he is looking for and what he is buying. You need to really open it up – a sales framework but allowing fan sites and niche players in to build up the superiority of your channel over others. Then you really have a winner.

Interactive TV is a great way of bringing the internet to those who don't want it. But it still doesn't personalize the service nearly enough. Service providers know who is using their service via the smart card that the e-customer slots in. Why don't they at least greet the e-customer by name? He pays the bills and if he notices the TV talking to him he is much more likely to interact with it. Interaction is just another step towards transaction and relationship.

Interactive TV offers the facility to list favourite channels, but surely it should compile the list automatically and remind the e-customer when they are on? It should use the information to make offers. Perhaps a web cast about a topic that is of great interest based on what has been watched to date. Perhaps an advert just shown to those people who have watched a particular film. Or an advert from a general supplier that shows one product to one segment and another advert to another.

Maybe you should be paying the e-customer to watch your adverts in cash, discounts or points systems. If you match the advert to the need then it will not be unwanted, it will be appreciated. Back to prompting.

The evolution will continue until it will be possible to have variable product placement. A different object appearing on a table in a digitally shot sitcom depending on the interests of the target e-customer: a musical instrument; a film ticket; a camera. We will see what is relevant to our needs. Our heroes will always be using the device that I haven't quite bought yet.

The capabilities of the internet currently mainly available via the PC will ultimately flow on to all other channels. In this way, order tracking and all the other useful e-stuff will bring benefits to all e-customers via user interfaces that are simple to view, understand and use.

Anything that can be seen on the net will be ultimately available through the TV. There are likely to be little information frames under television programmes showing additional information at any point. The smart card that allows viewing will be used as an additional, secure payment system – viewing, browsing, and buying all subject to the same easy to use parental controls.

It isn't glossy. It isn't continuous. It isn't rich. Broadband will bring it from one angle, merging the best of TV and the web regardless of the device it is viewed through.

“ Merging the best of

In the blue corner ... the real world

In order to compete we need to consider the real-world experience. How good it can get. And how bad it can be.

Businesses keen to encourage potential e-customers to consider the virtual world as a substitute for the real world have sponsored a number of online living stunts. These include bigbrother.com, jennicam.org and dotcomguy.com .

Since 1 January 2000, 26-year-old DotComGuy, who legally changed his name for the exercise, has bought his necessities and luxuries exclusively online. He rented a Dallas town house and vowed never to venture past his tiny backyard.

DotComGuy receives 1.5 million visits a day to see his life and read his opinions on numerous online services. After a year online DotComGuy says he doesn't miss stepping out into the world to shop:

both worlds will allow you to deliver **a superior** overall service to the e-customer "

PEOPLE SAY 'WELL, YOU'RE **ISOLATING YOURSELF**, YOU'RE NOT **INTERACTING** WITH PEOPLE'. TRULY, THE **LAST** TIME YOU WENT SHOPPING, WAS YOUR **INTERACTION** WITH PEOPLE OF **ANY QUALITY?** YOU WERE IN A HURRY, YOU **DIDN'T WANT** TO TALK TO ANYBODY, YOU **DIDN'T WANT** TO WAIT IN LINE, AND YOU WERE PROBABLY IN AN EXPRESS LINE.

But then such sponsored oddities are not at all objective. They can forget that the real-world shopping experience can be rich and personal. The 97% of business conducted in the real world has benefits that must be understood if online businesses, including yours, are to compete effectively.

Merging the best of both worlds will allow you to deliver a superior overall service to the e-customer. One that he will appreciate. And one that your competitors will struggle to replicate.

Our research recorded many rich and personal interactions off-line. One such conversation took place in a little bookshop in a small town centre. Not the kind of place that is going to cause Barnes & Noble nightmares. But incorporating the best aspects of stores like this around the world can help them to move beyond their main online rivals.

One assistant was able to inform, discuss, and build relationships with three customers while looking out for shoplifters. She told one customer about the price of CDs, explained the benefits of the buy-back scheme, and exchanged the views of her mother on the merits of a particular author.

The truth is that both virtual and real-world shopping experiences occasionally show their extremes by being appalling or delightful. But most often they can be disappointing, a little lacklustre and uninspiring. The experiences are different and yet somehow very familiar.

E-commerce vs real world shopping

In the real world, customers complain about 'waiting for months for items to be in stock' and having to 'lug huge boxes from store to car'. In the virtual world, e-customers sigh when they have to 'put up with systems that crash on the point of ordering' or when they do not receive 'answers to their e-mails'.

Some have argued that e-commerce has been promoted by men who love gadgets more than shopping and indeed evidence suggests that as many as one in six men do hate shopping.[20] Men and women aged between 35 and 49 dislike it the most and find it difficult to fit into their busy schedules. Busy women who dislike shopping (15%) actually outnumber men (10.5%).

Some services can fit into the virtual world without any trouble. The box can swallow them up and replace all relevant aspects of the real world. Other real-world services and experience can be complemented by their electronic counterparts.

There are limitations. You cannot eat on the net but food can be delivered to your doorstep. You can't dance on the net but you can certainly flirt. It is even possible to see ways in which the essence of some real world experiences are uprooted and replanted online or at home through the net. For instance, parties at home ....

Real-world locations that deliver dull experiences will be the first to come under attack (electrical retailers, estate agents, banks). Many of offer these second-rate experiences that can be considerably enhanced in the virtual world.

The real world is not ideal for certain kinds of shopping. It's not helpful if you actually have to take heavy goods away with you, shop for something specific or shop quickly. It does offer you the pleasures of finding a parking spot, traffic congestion, or the public transport system. But sadly these pleasures are less and less appreciated by today's lifestyle focused e-customer.

This is where the real-world experience will have to start making a difference. It needs to do what the virtual world cannot. The real world must keep reinventing its purpose while trying to minimize its weaknesses. But it must not forget that it is different or it will attempt to compete with virtual shopping at a disadvantage.

Of course people will still want to shop. But people who frequently use the net to shop do not necessarily shop less in the real world as a result. They use one medium to meet certain needs and the other to meet other needs.

Show the e-customer that what he thinks he wants from the real world may no longer be available.[21] Focus on the undesirable parts of the real-world shopping experience from your e-customers' perspective and try to get paid for removing them from the e-customers' lives . Dissatisfaction ranks alongside perspiration as a key ingredient to innovation.

Even the most ardent shopper will crumble when faced with either no economic choice or when the internet becomes so linked to everyday life that it is no longer practically possible to separate internet and non-internet services.

"Advertising

Six senses working overtime

Not everything exists in an electronic form: an obvious but somewhat neglected fact. Underemphasized perhaps because for a new idea to succeed against the traditions of the past it must often be presented in extreme, hyped terms.

If an internet pioneer says 'it's just another way of sending messages' or 'it has its place alongside all existing forms of communication' he is unlikely to demand much attention. Instead it has been the more extreme electronic evangelist who has been quoted by some portions of the traditional media, happy to relay headline-worthy statements and just as happy to knock them down as unworkable in the next paragraph.

Building value that is appreciated by the e-customer involves delivering the greatest amount of experience in each purchase. Raw e-stuff has great attributes but it needs to be enriched. Like the difference between a postcard and an e-mail: one can be quicker, more personal and more up-to-date; the other is a part of where you were – a physical link between the sender and the recipient.

Giving e-brands real world presence

One of the curious trends we now see is the electronic world spawning real-world offspring. To some extent this has been the case for some time where the desire of an electronic brand to expand beyond its natural (current web-users-only) market has led to extensive and extreme advertising.

Advertising can only partially 'physicalize' an electronic brand. The next steps will be to consider the other situations, locations and senses relevant to the e-customer.

n only partially
'physicalize'
an electronic band 99

Let's wait for the opening of the first Amazon World. A flag ship, interactive, 3D, service experience, featuring authors, demonstrations and exhibits linked to new or best-selling books within each range – using real people, real shops and serving the e-customer in the flesh. The logical embodiment of its recent advertising slogan 'a real company in a virtual world'.

Virgin.com may find its way to this ideal combination of real and virtual through the rebirth of Our Price, the Virgin-owned retail music chain, as the newly announced V-shops. The changes may have been encouraged by reducing margins due to online sales but they present a fantastic opportunity. Virgin can showcase the virtual world in the real world. Lower advertising costs, an exciting introduction and education to electronic channels.

Coca-Cola has been running a marketing campaign in the Mediterranean that one could term 'whistle and shout'. It involves a team clad in Coca-Cola red t-shirts and caps storming into a shop armed with whistles. They commence their enthusiastic and deafening whistling and shouting while one of them explains that for every crate of coke you buy, one will now be given to you 'absolutely free'. The whistling and shouting continues until all shoppers give in and buy.

A nightmare, right? But used with care such techniques could give the e-brand that real-world presence. Imagine similar teams clothed in the sportal.com colours or wearing the icq.com flower logo on baseball caps running into your local supermarket, bus station or gym. It would leave you confident that you were dealing with real people with a particular culture and approach. (For dangers of hassling customers see p. 136).

Go to the supermarket. Conduct a little poll. Look for products of all kinds. Which kinds and which brands link their real world to the virtual world? And how many encourage that link through promotions or promises or information or post-sales support?

A growing number of magazines, advertisements and product packages feature these valuable bridges between the worlds. Do your products do the same? A great example was featured on cereal packets from cheerios.com which invited anyone with 'growable e-customers' (or kids) to log on and use an online parenting resource featuring a children's 'Growing Book'. Link made. E-customer hooked.

Elsewhere, networked businesses are already using the web-cam craze to make their normally invisible real world operations visible and connected to their e-customers. The real is somehow made far more real than the remote backwoods factories and back rooms have ever been before.[22]

The net as a secure place

The net can appeal to the e-customer's **sense of security.** It's the ultimate clinically clean experience. No need for walks in the dark across deserted car parks or running the gauntlet of gangs of disaffected youth. No risky visits to real-world clubs and city centres.

Contrary to the continuous net security scare stories in the backward parts of our old media, the net is a pretty safe place. Which is more than you can say for the real world. DotComGuy has not even come close to being mugged during his ongoing experiment.

As long as the gate between the real and virtual worlds is kept secure then you are simply safer dealing with the real world through electronic channels. But the novice e-customer is still very afraid. Mainly because he isn't in control. He doesn't know what is out there and he imagines a world of 'lions, tigers and bears'.

What do we do when someone is frightened? Reassure them. Hold their hands. Put an arm around them. Explain that what really seems scary is something that is easily explained. You gotta do the whole debunking thing.

So go for the familiar. I don't mean copying the design of every other website. I am talking finding creative parallels between what your e-customer knows and trusts and what he needs to accomplish in e-space. It requires a metaphor merger of the two worlds.

If you are smart you will have your website accredited to a recognized scheme. This is becoming a vital ingredient in becoming accepted and trusted by the e-customer. In an environment full of scare stories and genuine security lapses it is necessary to demonstrate that you are completely trustworthy.

For many e-customers there is only one commercial internet. All e-commerce tends to be lumped together. The channel is so new for the majority that they assume that a security breach or dubious practices on one site are representative of the whole.

So problems at the competition are not automatically beneficial. The recent attempts by failed internet retailers (like Toysmart.com) to sell off their e-customer lists and other information to third parties are damaging. In some cases they are trying to do so despite legal agreements with data-privacy accreditation agencies (in this case, TRUSTe). It will require industry-wide action to avoid the trust fabric of the medium being compromized.

Effective communication is vital, so that your e-customers accept that this stuff only happens elsewhere. That you are an exception. That they have made the right decision in trusting you. Open, honest rules and principles. Bottom to top integrity. Rapid admission of guilt and generous corrective action.

The proposition

'free'

"Because that's what **GOD INTENDED** when he created both the USA and the Internet.

FAST AND FREE"

Lawrence Robinson, Net Magazine, 2000

The wonderful world of 'free'

Many of the companies competing in the great, wide, internet expanses are hoping that the dictum 'there's no such thing as a free lunch' is still true. The logic behind so many web business ideas goes something like this:

1 Customers like free (or very cheap) things.

2 If we are free (or very cheap) e-customers will like us.

3 BUT we will still make money one day because:

• in the future we can start to charge more;

• other companies will pay us to talk to free-loving e-customers;

• our business will be so efficient that we can afford to charge less.

Does all this stack up? A look at some of the thinking behind these 'golden but unproven' e-principles can be valuable.

We could ask whether e-customers **like free (or very cheap) things?** And the answer is yes. If they like a product or a service anyway then most e-customers would prefer to pay less for it. But that's not the whole story.

Do e-customers like free things?

There are e-customers who like rarity, scarcity, showing off what other people do not have, cannot afford, or chose not to buy. These people are unlikely to be impressed by the free that is widely available to everyone. So sometimes free has to be either limited to a select audience or kept a secret so that no one knows whether a thing is free or not.

Customers love free things but not if it means the thing is of poor quality. They love lower prices but they may love them less if it means that the product is not well supported or service is patchy or they cannot get through on the product information helpline.

> **"** Customers **love** free things **but not** if it means the thing is of poor quality **"**

When is a bargain not a bargain? When it doesn't work, it doesn't fit, it doesn't wash, it doesn't save time. When it is more hassle than it is worth.

The value exchange proposition

Free can be a vital part of a market plan but it cannot replace the plan. In fact it demands greater attention than ever to what e-customers are really buying and what the business is really selling. That's the value exchange proposition and it must be at the heart of the e-customer strategy.

You may ask sensibly at this point, how can the e-customer really be *buying* anything if the product is free? And the answer you will figure out comes back to the exchange of value.

Money is only a really neat way of exchanging the product of our time for the product of other people's time. We use it because there are significant real-world problems in simply swapping what we make or do for what other people make or do.

In the dim, distant past, bartering was the thing. I raise cute little pigs and exchange my pigs for everything else I need. Bacon is swapped for milk. Pork chops are converted into bear-skin slippers. Maybe sometimes a group of villages gets together to swap our combined produce for something really important that none of us can bargain for on our own.

Clearly the limitations of bartering include the necessity of physically moving the goods from one owner to the other. This makes anything other than the local, direct swap a pretty difficult transaction. Bartering also means that the exchange can only be done right now and for 100% of the item. It is also difficult to store any part of the exchange for later or swap for only part of my produce (granularity).

Money has certain properties that make it ideal for lubricating the process of exchange. With money, the basis of trade was transformed. You could turn your time into stuff and swap your stuff for money. Then you could use the money to buy other people's stuff whenever you wanted to.

Once it got started, money just carried on rolling around the world. Money has proved to be an essential component of life with its anytime, anywhere characteristics. In many ways, the internet has very similar properties to money and provides improved solutions to the problems that money has traditionally solved.

Improvements include its granularity. Ever wondered what happened to the half-pence or half-cent coins? After inflation had its impact it became too small in value to be economic. It cost more to manage it, count it, make it and move it around than it was worth.

Money has its own costs and it has also developed within the practical limitations of its use – people want as few coins as possible weighing down their pockets so we try to keep the lowest value coin at a reasonable level.

The e-customer is already presented with a number of innovations that revolve around the basic concept of value exchange. In a sense, the net and the mighty technologies behind it allow people to return to the essential nature of trading.

For example, if you want someone to spend their time looking at your marketing literature, your sales pitch or your adverts, you might be willing to budget what is often called 'the cost of sale' in order to entice them.

Sometimes the money is spent on special offers, competitions and even 'free gifts'. More often though the 'cost of sale' is split up between the advertising world (agencies, graphics designers) and the media world (TV stations, publishers and billboard owners).

There are many good (and enduring) arguments to support this expenditure but the e-customer can expect to receive far more of the 'cost of sale' budget directly for spending. For example, loyalty-points schemes that pay the e-customer for merely looking at information about a product and then continue even after he has bought the product.

Or loyalty scheme currencies that can be collected in minute amounts and exchanged for real-world money or other products. That is the reality of electronic only currencies like Beenz.

And it is so much fairer and clearer than the advertising only model. A simple case of paying the prospective customer what you think his time to look at your advert is worth. The e-customer will appreciate your valuation of his time and so your first contact with the e-customer is therefore positive. You can pay only for the time of e-customers that fit your targeting model and you can identify the e-customer in order to be able to pay him.

But you always pay for something. You still buy into it. You are always selling, at the very least, an idea. In the future you hope that someone will pay for it. Without the rush to free services, many people would not have even tried the service.

Sky e-mails probably only cost the price of postage stamps but the cost itself is off-putting. If Sky wants to spread the net then they will have to lower the price or build a one-off cost into the subscription.

What to do with all that cash the e-customer is not spending
If the e-customer can buy it for zero cash elsewhere then he isn't going to pay for the same stuff from you, is he? More interestingly he's going to leave your competitors without reducing the cash that is sloshing around in his virtual pockets. Start figuring out what to do with all that money that the e-customer isn't spending on free stuff elsewhere. It has to go somewhere. Under the bed, in the bank, down the bookies. Why not help him spend it with you?

Will they take those cost savings and spend them on more cars, on technology or spend them elsewhere in the economy? Will they choose to have another holiday or have more meals in restaurants. Be the beneficiary of all this extra cash! Sing along with me:

HE'S BUSY SPENDING NOTHING. **BROWSING** THE WHOLE DAY THROUGH.

TRYING TO FIND **LOTS OF THINGS NOT TO DO.**

HE'S BUSY GOING NOWHERE, **ISN'T IT SUCH A CRIME.**

HE'D LIKE TO SPEND HIS MONEY BUT HE

NEVER DOE

The net itself will create winners and losers but not in the automatic way that many start-up dot.commers imagine. The costs will be sucked out of the initial web targets. Suppliers will be squeezed. Margins removed.

Make sure that your stuff is worth more to the e-customer than it costs to provide. Services need to be designed that can increase the e-customer's average order size and sell higher margin products while avoiding discounting. They need to use the power of the electronic channels *together* with other marketing channels. Make your reputation more meaningful than a third-party brand and your margins can grow further.

Focusing on total e-customer numbers may keep the investors and shareholders at bay for a while but it will not bring profits. Experience shows that the losses based on variable costs of supplying an item are as much as $12 per item because of the low margins, low order sizes, and high cost of delivery. Given the choice, opt for services that have high total e-customer values. Retail categories like online groceries, prescription drugs and speciality clothing will bring up to 200% more revenue per e-customer than internet only books, clothing, toys or music.[23]

Propositions need to attract those who are willing to pay. Don't worry about overall e-customer numbers. Throwing money in the air will attract everyone. What you need is to sell tickets to quality events and then count the profits. This is the way to create loyal, profitable relationships. Research shows that about a third of the customers bring in two-thirds of the profits.[24] Avoid forcing the real buyers to subsidize your marketing to those who only want it if it's free or loss leading.

HAVE THE TIME

Services that require direct payment are growing on the net. They can fund their own growth by attracting e-customers to a service where the fee actually covers the cost.[25] The only way to make money will be in added additional services that people are happy to pay for. And you better make your services difficult to replicate or some guy working for the competition will copy them and then give them away as well.[26]

The housekeeper question

So how much of your privacy are you willing to give up in order to receive more personalized products and services? The technology now exists to track every move the e-customer makes. This is possible because every move he makes creates an electronic footprint that can be recorded and analyzed.

This is very similar to the butler, personal assistant or housekeeper question. The benefit of personal service is that it should respond to your every need and adapts to your every whim. The price to be paid is that you must allow someone to understand your needs, schedule, peculiarities and whims.

This requires trust. The e-customer must believe that the company, to whom he gives his details and permission to track every interaction and purchase, will:

• Keep the data safe and private.

• Use the data effectively in his interest to improve his lifestyle.

If you want to offer such a personalized business to the e-customer (we will talk about the advantages of personalization in a moment), the best approach is to work on building a trustworthy service and then communicating your trustworthiness to the e-customer.

And there's another thing. The style of the delivery of a product 'made just for you' has to be a style that is 'made just for you'. Sometimes the delivery is more valuable than the product.

Such has been the reduction in personal servants that most of our images of those who serve us personally come from literature and film. This is immensely appealing when in the form of Alfred Pennyworth, the unflappable butler, effortlessly protecting his master who is the millionaire Bruce Wayne and vigilante Batman.

The problem comes in the worrying shape of such icons as Manuel, the hapless Spanish waiter from cult UK comedy *Fawlty Towers*. Would you trust him with any of your secrets? Tell him what you want and you can expect the opposite.

Using personal information to meet the needs of your e-customer

Who is going to be that trusted keeper of information? The manufacturer? The intermediary? A personal shopper? Or an organization that does nothing but store personal information so that others can use it to meet your needs more accurately.

This latter role (winwin.com) is one that will continue to grow because:

- It is a competence that extends across individual businesses.

- Many organizations are not skilled at keeping and using information at the individual level.

- People do not want to keep giving their information out again and again. That removes the advantage of using an electronic system.

Some people will opt out of the personalization movement because they would prefer to escape the corporate web rather than escape the world of duplicated effort.[27] These are not natural e-customers! But there are some who are borderline who have concerns that are surmountable.

Trusted third parties will provide access to information, verify age, status and ensure that payments are secure. It is far from clear whether all these services will be provided by just one business or whether they will continue to be divided out among other specialists. In the short term, they will proliferate like store loyalty cards: each scheme promising much, with consumers signing up for many and using them only sporadically. It is hard even to remember the rules or which ones I belong to after a while.

Credit agencies have for some time played a role that is similar to that of the trusted keeper of information. They work by collecting public information from a variety of sources and combine it with private credit information from their clients about their e-customers. This is different in significant ways because they do not have to ask for the

"The data is just the beginning "

information and it works for businesses to help them avoid
untrustworthy e-customers.

For some, less well-prepared organizations, just organizing the
e-customer data into one place is tricky enough. In almost every major
business in the world there is either a 'data warehousing' project or a
'customer relationship management' project. These projects are not, on
the whole, fantastic successes. Many have failed even to escape the
interminable meetings trap.

They should just get a grip and get it sorted. The data is just the
beginning. After it is all connected it has to be used to serve the
e-customer more effectively.

It's not that hard to figure out what the e-customer wants. He wants
what rich people have had for millennia: services and experiences that
have remained the province of the rich because of the manpower
required to provide them.

So we want personal trainers, cooks, gardeners. And now technology
can combine to deliver these to a wider market than was previously
possible by allowing us a 'timeshare' of that individual. At a rate that is
economical for us. At a price that is profitable for the business.

Take the personal trainer example. What does the e-customer really
want from a personal trainer? He doesn't care whether they are there in
person in his home. He wants personal advice and encouragement
when he is ready to train. Someone who is aware of his exercise
regime. Someone who can watch his form and ensure that he

completes his repetitions. Someone he can ask about diet, posture and health.

The increased availability of web cams (inexpensive video cameras that link to a computer), computers and free internet access should open up the possibility of the time-shared personal trainer. Someone from whom the e-customer receives individual attention at home or in the gym.

It's one to one. One on one. It's personalized. But the trainer can be in more than one place simultaneously and he doesn't need to waste time travelling.

Of course once the process and the technology platform have been set up it is a service that suddenly becomes portable. International. Convenient. The perfect executive service.

One billion e-customers?

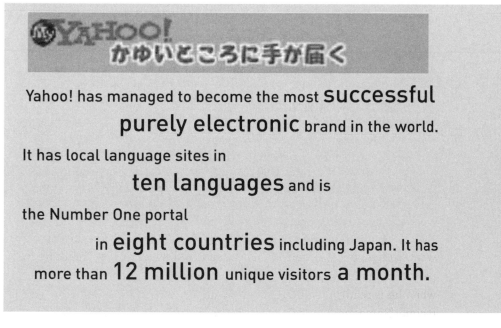

Yahoo! has managed to become the most **successful purely electronic** brand in the world.

It has local language sites in **ten languages** and is the Number One portal in **eight countries** including Japan. It has more than **12 million** unique visitors **a month**.

Globalization. It makes you laugh. Distance died in 1989 according to pundits and here we are with sites that still don't recognize foreign post codes or allow you to purchase if you don't live in the same country. Opportunity? You bettcha.

There are a lot of people who don't live in your country or speak your mother tongue.[28] There are even more who don't share your tastes or opinions in politics, clothes, sporting idols or popular music. But you need to get beyond that if you are to reach past your limited natural constituency.

Sometimes your home market will not be the most lucrative. It may be that your home base and starting point is not your natural or optimum market. Why scrabble around in a local market of 1 or 2% of the population when you could be selling into a market of 50%?

Scale is impressive as long as you can count on the benefits of volume and presence. For millennia, those who really want to make it big have travelled the world to conquer each others' territories. Don't make the mistake of shutting your doors on a wallet brandishing e-customer just because he happens to be in the wrong country. There should never be a wrong country.

There is no wrong country to be in if you are a fan of Whitney, The Back Street Boys or Ricky Martin. They are far more (or less) than pop artists. They are global marketing creations with international appeal. You, like them, can choose to deliver an international message (locally translated) while still delivering essentially the same service.

Alternatively you can learn your lessons from the internationalization of rap. It has crept into multiple nations and languages. It shares the same attitudes, clothes, bass beat and rhythmic vocal delivery but has evolved to the point that it is as relevant to local culture as it is to that of US ghettos.

Expansion via electronic channels does not have to consider markets as primarily geographic or even linguistic. It can look at them as 'lifestyle' based, selling the service to anyone with a similar set of needs, problems or aspirations. The trick is in communicating those benefits to your potential e-customer.

Remember that communication requires certain compatibilities. Like language. Or slang. Let's not forget attitude. And culture. Hobbies. Background. All the things that make each person different from some people and similar to others.

As the net widens, the natural similarities between those caught up in it become slightly less obvious. No longer automatically technophile and early adopter. Not necessarily from middle-class homes. Not forcibly wealthy. Less likely than ever to be a geek 'cyberpunk' wannabee.

Early adopters of the web were weird. They were also bound together by common interests and intelligence. But this is no longer the case. It cannot be depended upon to allow you to deliver unvaried content.

Speak your e-customer's language

The e-customer prefers to speak in his own language. It's more comfortable, it's more accurate and it puts him at ease. It's easier to sell when the communication is designed for him: tone, speed, vocabulary, approach, aligned to the e-customer so that he knows that the message is for him.

" The e-customer **prefers to speak** in his own language "

Consider language as just such a common need. Spanish provides a bond between most of Latin America, Spain and the US Hispanic population. Reaching out to the faster growing segments is an attractive step if Latin American and Spanish businesses are to compete on equal terms.

Listen to how impressed Luciana Arraes, a Brazilian e-customer, was when her purchase (from cdnow.com) was followed up in her own language:

I RECEIVED AN E-MAIL **IN PORTUGUESE**, AND UNTIL THAT MOMENT THEY HAD **NEVER ASKED ME** WHICH WAS **MY LANGUAGE.** AND MORE THAN THAT THE PERSON **WHO** SIGNED THE MESSAGE **DIDN'T BELONG** TO THE SALES DEPARTMENT AND YES IT WAS **A PERSON!**

You think that maybe the experience has brought Luciana closer to her supplier? Even when the e-customer can cope in another language he will appreciate you making the effort to respond in his mother tongue. It's a powerful tool. And one that is easier to do electronically than any other way.

Rather than reach out to the world, a business can choose to wait until the world learns its particular local language. It may feel that its local market is large enough. You may be tempted to agree – unless you are thinking about being a truly global company. Unless you would prefer to avoid being dwarfed by too many competitors growing to behemoth size in every other language zone before coming to gobble you up. That's a real danger.

It's great to feel superior in your own area. In your own locale. Much of the English-speaking world is feeling pretty smug. It is master of the magical language of the internet. All it needs to do is wait for the rest of the world to catch up.

But if you sail only in familiar linguistic waters you will be cut off from most of the world. For the anglophone world it's easy to assume that if 70% of the world's internet content is in English then e-customers will be prepared to cope. But focus on English and you *still* have only half a billion native English readers.

You will still be neglecting the 332 million Spanish, 170 million Portuguese and 1 billion Chinese readers. Not forgetting the other 6 billion potential e-customers on Earth. Don't worry you could get lucky. The rest of the world may just sit there learning English. Your markets may grow as each e-customer graduates from their online English course.

You could leave international e-customers to the mercies of online dictionaries and lexicons like 'Traduttore' from the Italian portal tiscalinet.it They may even find new services like those offered by Babylon.com (Israel) that allow single-word translation or the Babelfish service from altavista.com that translates web pages in real time as the e-customer browses. These are all ways for the rest of the world to enjoy a virtual world so much larger than its own.

The e-customer may speak any one of the 2,700 languages in the world and it's no good waiting for them all to die out. In the book *Vanishing Voices*, Daniel Nettle and Suzanne Romaine estimate that by 2100 half of the world's languages will be extinct.[29] Would you like to wait that long?

Even if it happens it will take another 200 years. And the bicentenary business plan is not something that even the net-foolish will buy. To compete at a global level requires local content. It requires local sensibilities and local personalization. A point that is well made in the copy of the following advertisement:

THE KIMS ARE **DEEPLY INTERESTED** IN KOREAN HISTORY.

YOUR CUSTOMER HELP DESK **RECOMMENDED** THEY READ THE MING DYNASTY

AND **MEMOIRS OF A GEISHA.** IS YOUR CUSTOMER SERVICE PROGRAM

IN A CULTURE **SHOCK?**

This kind of cultural ignorance will make efforts to create services that mould profitably around the e-customer fruitless. The full set of e-customer characteristics must be considered and met.

Consider the Latin American situation where service providers are figuring out how they can use their resources to conquer the 3.1 million US Hispanics. They are busy buying up companies that extend their reach – young upstarts and old-timers that have fallen a tad off the pace, as typified by the newly launched terralycos.com.

The challenge will be in how well they can reach out beyond the language to meet the local needs and interests of new markets. The existing super-hip content providers are typically scathing. They know that they understand the market but they may overestimate the value of their knowledge. Consider the opinion of Carlos Lizarralde, of Miami-based Loquesea.com:

A LOT OF LATIN AMERICAN COMPANIES **ARRIVING OVERNIGHT** ARE

TOTALLY CLUELESS ON HOW TO REACH THIS **MYTHICAL MARKET**.

IT'S THE **TOUGHEST MARKET** IN THE WORLD BECAUSE THE

HISPANIC KIDS DO NOT WANT **REFRIED CONTENT** FROM LATIN AMERICA

AND **DO NOT IDENTIFY** WITH OLD-LINE, OFF-LINE **HISPANIC MEDIA**

IN THE US.

Of course Hispanic kids do not want refried content but content can be locally injected into existing global operations and systems. It is a relatively simple matter to recruit local editors and writers. Or to sign content provision deals with existing magazines, newspapers and websites.

It's going to take the sophisticated efforts of technologists, local content creators, process designers and editors. Don't just aim for a thoughtless culling of staff numbers. You may need just as many people but in different areas serving more and more focused e-customer groups.

Speaking the e-customer's language also involves considering differences beyond those existing between national cultures. National differences are vitally important but the key differences of the next 30 years will be between lifestyle groupings.

This is not a prediction of world peace or bland homogeneity. There will nevertheless be a significant proportion of the world who will share beliefs, interests, tastes, information sources and social preferences with others across national boundaries.

The way to produce content that 'clicks' is to have it created by those who share perspectives with the e-customers that you serve. This can mean partnerships with providers (magazines, e-zines and newspapers) that have proven appeal. This is how you will build genuine relationships and discover local niches for your existing services.

It can also mean actually employing people to serve your e-customers who would naturally be part of one of your target groups. It's an approach that has been effectively utilized in the real world by the UK retailing group Selfridges. 'Vitorio Radice, CEO, removed the uniform. Teenagers got teenager shop assistants with tattoos, and the sports departments got Australian jocks with pierced noses in Nikes.'[30] It just makes sense so don't fight it. You need a balanced workforce to deliver the best service to a balanced group of e-customers. This is the opposite of most recruitment approaches and outcomes.

Tone needs to match the natural tone of the groups that you are serving, the particular tone of the individuals within those groups, and the mood of the moment. Sometimes the e-customer just wants to get things done or play for a while. If you can adapt to him then he will become more comfortable and list you as his kind of place. So learn to speak his language.

Something with a soul

The net has been accused of being soul less, of lacking that warmth that we seek in our daily human interactions. Electronic channels have been created by humans but are often not created for them. Pleasing the e-customer will require devices and services that have been created for people with the e-customer in mind from the start.

214 different hands.
72 different bands.
6 different shapes.
7 **1 million** colours different materials.
200 million units sold.
swatch has made
its fortune by creating stuff that people can love.
And **now** they are hunting the e-customer. Will they **catch him?** It's the internet on your **wrist.**

In with at least a good chance of capturing e-customer hearts and minds is Swatch. Led by the design philosophy 'create something with soul', it has managed to transform itself, from crisis-stricken watch industry to creator of personality products (my term) that have already sold over 200 million units. Consider one of its recent innovations. Its founder and visionary, Nicolas Hayek, and his team have understood the need to place Swatch at the centre of the internet. In partnership with

Nicolas Negroponte, famed MIT futurist, it has even a time system suitable for a global internet. It has done so by dividing up the virtual and real day into 1,000 'beats' which leaves 12 noon in the old time system as the equivalent of @500 Swatch beats. No time zones. The perfect time system for the e-customer.

It has since considered how to ensure that the internet is focused on its heartland between forearm and hand by developing the 'Swatch internet browser' and the 'Swatch context aware' watch that uses GPS to show different information dependent on the location of the e-customer.

Designers would be advised to do far more story-boarding. Imagine how the service will be used in the real word. Figure out how to make a difference that the e-customer will appreciate. Just launching the service may be an achievement in the lives of your team but it will not register for the e-customer unless it makes a recognizable difference to their day-to-day life.

When Jonathan Ives pursued his mission of humanizing the computer by creating the iMac he was after something with a soul. He wanted to create a key tool to give digital power to anyone. The iMac is excitingly people focused, with its 'emotional human form' design. In his words:

GO WITH THE BELIEF THAT YOU **CAN DO IT BETTER, SIMPLER** AND **MORE ELEGANTLY.** THEN YOU CAN CAPTURE THE HEARTS AND **MINDS OF PEOPLE**, AND JUST AS IMPORTANT, THEIR WALLETS. **IT'S A VICTORY FOR EVERYONE.**

In designing stuff and services with soul, you will need to assume that radically better *is* possible. That's what Kozo Ohsone, Sony's manufacturing guru, did to create the Walkman. It was a landmark piece of phenomenally effective alignment between e-customer lifestyle and technology advances.

It was made possible by following his nine commandments that include 'just saying OK, without considering the ramifications' and 'learn to live with the impossible'. Internet-based services can be moulded around the e-customer, they can be made indispensable. But it is a very, very difficult thing to do. And it requires the suspension of normal constraints and approaches.

To create something that changes lifestyles you have to think of the desirable and make it feasible. It does not have to be feasible when you begin. Others may dismiss the idea. Like the Yale professor who gave Fred Smith, the founder of Federal Express, a C for his paper that proposed the idea of overnight delivery because 'to earn better than a C, the idea must be feasible'.

Just look up the value of FedEx today. And Sony.

It's worth pondering. Worth considering until it sinks in. You cannot offer lifestyle improvements to the e-customer simply by repeating what has already been done. That's okay if you want to rely on market flukes or your corporate bulk to get you by. It might work. It might not. Hey it's only your career. You may even have enough money to never work again. But where is the satisfaction in just limping along?

The grape-nut story

So. The grape-nut story. Stuff that we can't buy easily anymore in the local mall. Stuff that we grew up with. Stuff that our grandparents remember. Stuff with childhood resonance. These meaningful brands that have disappeared from our lives and stores for some reason.

Some of these items are available on the net. Other dim and dusty brands could find themselves reinvigorated through drinking at the well of all things direct. The net allows the niche to become smaller (narrower) and the niche becomes bigger (greater potential audience). So 1% of the cereal sales for one supermarket in one nation is not a lot. Perhaps not enough to keep you on the shelves. Perhaps not enough to keep you in business.

But 1% of ten nations' entire cereal consumption. Direct to their doors. Cutting out sales costs to supermarkets. Restoring margins to the manufacturer. That may change the economics of reviving a beloved old brand.

An e-mail campaign for such a brand via an existing internet brand. A 'do you remember when' campaign for grape-nuts. An animated slice of nostalgia. Inviting them to click to order a direct delivery. Grape-nuts at your doorstep the very next day.

The lost and forgotten years. Makes a lot of sense on the net. It builds on the trend for sites dedicated to hobbies, trivia, obsessions and collectables. Thrash metal from the Midwest. Amateur websites not making any money. But they show the level of grass roots interest in stuff that has died in the real world.

The afterlife phenomenon of the virtual world can be combined with the low fixed distribution and marketing costs to bring about brand resurrection. Many have withered away because of the cost of advertising and marketing, and the natural predilection of chains to favour the strong rather than the weak when deciding how to fill a finite number of shelves.

But in the virtual world the shelves go on for ever. And they are all just a search away. The products may not sell as many as those sold in the supermarket but they are still making money. Strip away usual costs and you may discover unusual levels of profitability.

Marketing then sits around the brand. Authenticity wrapped up in authentic community, services, gimmicks and information. Niches that can be tested. Marketing evidence that may be used to re-emerge into the real world. Or grass roots. Invisible success stories for those who like things just they way they were. It's the potential value of the net. The niche-brand portfolio.

Usually commerce and journalism are about making tough decisions about what to leave out, what to stock and what to print. You are unlikely to be able to stock everything and, even if you could, the size of the store would make the shopping experience more akin to heavy-duty cross-country training.

This means, of course, that you are missing out a load of business, but such decisions are the nature of business. It's why large businesses tend to gravitate towards the middle ground, assuming that at least if the products are average then they will be bought. Then when e-customers buy them (unable to find alternatives they settle on the average) the conclusion is that the purchasing decision was right.

So hold on just a moment. Are we saying that if there was a way of stocking an infinite range of information *and* products and allowing the e-customer to select easily what they want it would open those untapped markets back up?

Yup. That's the beauty of electronic channels.

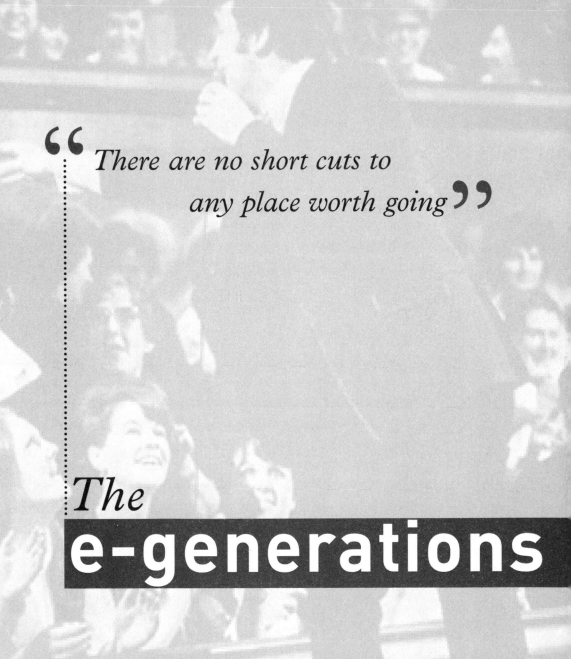

" *There are no short cuts to any place worth going* **"**

The
e-generations

This revolution has a history

The e-commerce surge did not just happen. We have not witnessed a simple process of invention and adoption over only a few years. This revolution has a history, a precedent, a story. And it is by looking at this story that we can better understand what this process will do to the business of serving the e-customer.

Valuable insights are to be gained by looking at the generations that have created, worked and then innovated with what has become our present-day virtual world. Each has had its inventors, fashions and social norms. These are intertwined and can only be understood when considered together.

Born during the first 40 years of the last century, the new and silent generations came into a world where 'youngers' listened to elders, children were seen and not heard, where the socio-economic status quo was at least given lip service. It was also the generation that witnessed the serious movement into the connected age. Radio (1895) and telephone (1876) started to be adopted into the mainstream but progress was slow. The facsimile machine (teleprinter, 1907) would wait a further 60 years before being considered an everyday piece of equipment.

Boomers (1921–40) found themselves in the middle of hugely significant political upheaval dominated by events surrounding the two world wars. Growing up, they were more aware than ever of a world outside their own local community.

Generation X (1961–80), according to the pundits and historians, have tended to grow up with little hope for the future, the way it was going, and no one at home when they returned from school. This has been the catalyst for their individualism and resourcefulness.

It has thrown up some of the key entrepreneurial computing heroes, including Jeff 'no profits' Bezoz, Bill 'obscene profits' Gates, Steve 'mouse prophet' Jobs, and Marc 'where did all the profits go?' Andresson. Their respective organizations have defined the software world the e-customer inhabits.

"All the great business ventures have by fluke or design met a need"

Generation Y includes anyone born after 1981. There are more than 2.4 billion of them in the world. The last of Generation Y will arrive on the planet on 31 December 2001. This is the group that have grown up with modern computing devices. The first point-and-click computer (Apple Lisa) was announced the year that their parents were celebrating their new arrivals.

The internet was more than ten years old when they were born. They have grown up at the same time and reached adolescence together. A gap has been apparent for the first decade, where money made all the difference in determining whether you had direct access to the net or to computers. But for more and more of this generation advanced computing power has been available in the home, school or cyber café.

They get online and get together with their friends in real-time conversations supported by typed text, video and graphical chat environments. They take 'personalized everything' as normal (like the jean production at 2gen.com). They are accused of being disrespectful, materialistic and selfish. They take the net for granted and are integrating it with their lifestyles. An automatic, natural extension.

The next generation, Generation Z, will come kicking and screaming on to the scene as from 1 January 2002. They will arrive surrounded by networked technology. They will play with robotic toys (not all of them of course, but many of them). Plugged in kids who take wireless multimedia for granted and are educated using automated internet tutors.

And they are all e-customers. They all hold secrets and insights into what the virtual world can, should and will deliver. The history is important and so is each age group and sub-culture.

All the great business ventures have by fluke or design met a need. The time between inventing stuff and its exploitation appears to be shortening because the inventor-entrepreneur has arrived. But the ideal application of the networked technologies and concepts of the past 100 years has not yet been achieved.

That is the prize that awaits anyone who cares to think long enough and creatively enough about just what each generation and their inventions tell us.

Me-inc.com

The e-customer wants to look good and feel good. Accept the challenge of making him look better and feel better! There is so much scope in us all for improvement. It's a well that will never run dry. And that's a good thing.

Already the net has examined dating and romance, dress and grooming, career, education, family, peace of mind and health. It has also inspired millions of websites created to reflect the e-customer's personality, interests and desire to be heard.

The e-customer experiences his 15 seconds of fame as strangers or fellow enthusiasts drift in and out of his strange little world, leaving behind comments in his visitor's book and adding just one more to his site counter.

The phenomenon of personality or vanity websites is also firmly established. Think of a famous person and there are usually official or unofficial websites (lennoxlewis.com or cindy.com). When there isn't a website then the site name will have been registered as some 'cyber-squatter' waits for his reward.

This focus on self has even made the transition to what

is known as 'ego surfing', a term featured in the *Oxford English Dictionary* since 1998, where the e-customer searches for occurrences of his own name. Of the 3,000 people that voted in a recent online survey run by zdnet.com more than 50% admitted that they had carried out such a search.

For some it is about vanity, for others a desire to be accessible to the world. According to Gary Stock, the creator of egosurf.com, most find themselves surprised and a few come back disappointed:

MOST EGO SURFERS **DISCOVER** SOME PIECE OF **INFORMATION** ABOUT THEMSELVES THAT THEY HAD **NO IDEA** APPEARED ANYWHERE. PEOPLE HAVE NO IDEA **HOW MANY TIMES** THEY TURN UP SOMEWHERE ON THE WEB. SOME PEOPLE GO OUT EXPECTING TO SEE THEMSELVES **ALL OVER THE PLACE** AND FIND NO MATCHES AT ALL. **LET ME TELL YOU,** LOOKING FOR YOURSELF AND FINDING NOTHING CAN BE A **REAL BLOW TO THE EGO.**

The idea that the web fulfils the e-customer's need to represent himself is supported by the continuing growth in the use of home pages – up over the past two years from 25% of the internet population to 50%. A whole industry has developed from giving the e-customer his own little patch in the virtual world.

Others are recognizing how the need for identity is linked to the need for recognition in building commercial relationships. Products and services are springing up that are capable of allowing the e-customer to construct his own space that incorporates the commercial offerings of the business.

The word 'My' is starting to be the first sign that an electronic service has decided to support the e-customer on his terms. This includes My

" It's **got** to be a good idea to

of an e-customer

Yahoo!, My Lycos, My Amazon and My Bank. Each service allows the e-customer to customize news, colours, personal information and images. Many allow the e-customer to add his own photos, text and documents. Others even allow the e-customer to benefit from sales that come via his content.[31]

It's got to be a good idea to combine the enthusiasm of an e-customer for a particular subject with sales of stuff that is related to that subject. It's also possible to take the concept even further and build a business where the content depends entirely on the opinions of e-customers.

This is the case with epinions.com, whose self-proclaimed mission is to help people make better buying decisions by providing e-customers with the facility to expose the good and the bad about products they have tested and get paid for sharing their expertise. Lane Becker, an e-customer from Florida who subverted the system to review epinions.com itself, comments:

BUT THEN, ALSO, THERE'S SOMETHING ABOUT THE IDEA: **LETTING PEOPLE WRITE,** LETTING PEOPLE **EXPRESS THEMSELVES,** LETTING PEOPLE **CONNECT** OVER CONTENT, IN A FORM THAT'S MEANINGFUL – ALBEIT COMMERCIAL, AND COMMERCIALLY ORIENTED, BUT **WHO ARE WE KIDDING?** THAT'S WHAT MOST PEOPLE REALLY **CARE ABOUT,** WHAT MOST PEOPLE REALLY – FEEL DEEPLY – ABOUT, RIGHT? **THEIR STUFF.** IN AMERICA, I MEAN. **GOD BLESS AMERICA,** DID I MENTION?

combine the **enthusiasm**

for a **particular subject** with sales

of stuff that is related to that subject "

And epionions.com is just part of a new breed of e-services that create trust and revenue (it gets paid through advertising and anything bought through its site) through utilizing the opinions of its e-customers. E-customers can be paid for their answers to questions at answerpoint.ask.com.

Other electronic services need to focus on enhancing the e-customer's social life. Here the e-customer would appreciate not only traffic congestion alerts but information about a whole range of potential situations that are best avoided. The boring colleague two offices down from him. The guy that wants to sell him insurance. Avoiding such meetings might be a more than worthwhile use of location based services.

Already in Japan there is a device that stores your ideal companion preferences. If you walk past someone else who matches your interests and who is carrying a similar device it will make a noise alerting you to stop and talk.

No more sitting silently on a train, bus or in a waiting room travelling elsewhere to meet people. Instead the device will alert you that you are sitting next to a valuable business contact, fellow golf addict or parent whose child also suffers from asthma.

There are so many similarities between people. If computers could alert us to what they are we would start off our conversations with more memorable subjects than travel and the weather.

Technology that helps the e-customer to make friends rather than locking him into his office? Now you're talking.

Building services around the e-customers

The question is not whether technology is capable of delivering the components but whether businesses are capable of figuring out how the components should be combined. They need to care enough to think about business from the e-customer's perspective. They need to understand the technology enough to see the possibilities and think beyond them. Will they gain the skills and training needed to build services around the e-customer?

It's the concept of dressme.com (not a real site yet) – keeping the e-customer's picture online. An upload or a web-cam snap. A little virtual him. On record with the facilities to play with colours, hair styles, make-up, hats and clothes. Providing the ability to try on different outfits in virtual reality.

Joe 90

Or the concept of whereami.com, prompting the e-customer to go and see a shop that had attracted his attention in the past when he is again in the vicinity. Or to call a certain person that he had always meant to call when there is a gap in his timetable. Task management systems that work to fit his prioritized tasks into his schedule instead of being yet one more task to fit into his busy life.[32]

The e-customer is looking for the type of functionality that allows him to upload his CV and improve it or create a new one with online tools. That connects him with his own career advisor who works one-to-one and in the background to match him with appropriate training and vacancies. That gives him aptitude tests and coaching right up to the last moment before an exam or interview.

Online education is becoming big business and an important self-improvement tool. Quicker, more convenient and cheaper than its real-world equivalents. Such services fit neatly into the e-customer's desire to achieve more. One of them, acadio.com, claims that it will:

GIVE CONSUMERS THE **OPPORTUNITY** TO QUICKLY AND EASILY FIND,

EVALUATE, COMPARE, AND PURCHASE **LEARNING** PRODUCTS AND SERVICES.

IT WILL PROVIDE **VALUABLE** INFORMATION AND RESOURCES TO BUILD

STRENGTHS, SHARPEN SKILLS, FOCUS DIRECTION, AND

EXPAND LIFE EXPERIENCES, GIVING PEOPLE THE **EDGE** THEY NEED

TO **IMPROVE** THEIR LIVES.

Joe 90 glasses. Plugging you into a world of information. Millions of Palm Pilots. Information following you about to support your life, your aspirations, and your lifestyle. All of these are possible. And they really could revolutionize the world of shopping and maybe even the world of being you.

Pester power

E-kid was born with the internet in his blood. In a world of Splat, Cheesy Strings, Pokémon and the Cartoon Network. For children, it will be the convergence of fads and their associated merchandizing that will pull their purchasing power on to the electronic stage.

They are already determining the fate of each new pop act just as their parents and grandparents did in their teens. Fashion and consumerism are established kindergarten pastimes. There is no sign of this changing.

Where teens were once the lucrative target market and king-makers, the e-kid has now emerged to do the very same. They don't need to pester you for money because they already have so much of yours. They love S-Club-7 and would have thought that Bucks Fizz and the Osmonds were cool.

Girls with hair clips, bands and nail varnish. All dolled up and into clothes and into music at seven years old. Boys and girls obsessed with networked, multi-player games via their PC or Games Console. Mobile phone text flirting in the classroom at ten years old. It's a kid's world.

Pester power. This a cute one. Linking stuff that children are interested in and the net. They learn very quickly. It is easier to memorize a web address than a telephone number anyway. And you can really link the brand colour, style and interactivity between real and virtual worlds. You can link entertainment, education and the next sale. They get it. Just listen to one seven year old:

I THINK IT IS **REALLY USEFUL** THAT IF YOU SEE A QUIZ ON TV YOU CAN USE THE INTERNET TO GIVE THEM AN ANSWER OR **ASK ANOTHER QUESTION.** THAT'S REALLY USEFUL. I THINK THAT IT IS **REALLY GOOD** THAT PEOPLE PUT WEBSITES ON THINGS THAT YOU **USE OR BUY IN EVERYDAY LIFE** LIKE CEREAL PACKETS, YOU GET THEM ON **POKÉMON CARDS,** ON TOYS, LOTS OF PLACES.

THAT'S WHERE I GET THEM FROM.

This requires community. Partnership. Something extra. Something special to reward kids for coming online. A secret thing. They love that approach. The Famous Five. The Secret Seven. Just think Enid Blyton, J.K. Rowling and every secret agent kit ever sold.

Just think of the possibilities
Go further. Think through children's eyes and be surprised when you discover that their view of the net is more advanced than your own. Brainstorm your way up the average level of the e-kid. Introduce child-

moderated chat rooms, some kind of game linked to your brand like an interative version of Pokémon with unique ID numbers of the backs of your products.

They should have it all. Themed shopping. A way of children seeing everything possibly linked to their particular fad, interest or obsession. Instead of an e-retailer having rows and rows of toys. Every toy-buying experience being the same. Having to move in towards the toy that you want with a series of clicks along a hierarchical series of hyperlinks or searching for the toy of interest. Themed shopping builds an experience around a particular toy range: process, content, games and links all integrated to reflect the interests of the range of toys being bought.

Imagine the attraction of a homework site featuring competitions to win Harry Potter books, pencil cases and Pokémon cards. Implement facilities to allow recommendations, referrals and web rings. The beauty of linking children's interests is that they tend to share common waves of interest (fads) much more predictably.

Use the backs of cereal packets and toys to build common loyalty-point systems. Many existing loyalty points and special offers are difficult to redeem. That's a problem for e-customer and vendor because neither party benefits and loyalty is not encouraged if the scheme is not used.

There are already loyalty schemes but not those that link the real world and the virtual world. We need schemes that track and guide the e-customer regardless of channel. Kiosks that demonstrate products and contain relevant information about them should also allow an e-customer to swipe his card and receive bonus points in exactly the same way as he is rewarded online for browsing certain sites related to schemes like Thingworld and Beanies.

A trail between channels and sites. A treasure hunt. The Pokémon trail. An extension of web rings leading from one kid-friendly site, channel or store to the next. Bonus points accruing to the child if his parent buys in particular stores or buys certain products.

Free sign-up for a loyalty card on the net. Loyalty cards in cereal packets that children could then present when their parents buy certain clothes, books, games or toys. Perhaps even extending the scheme to include parent purchases like cars, food or holidays. The parent may not have any preference which brand to buy, and so pester power accentuated by points could just tip the balance.

Children love raising money for charities, saving the world, book clubs, catalogues brought home from school. Perhaps the amazons of the world should be sponsoring or even buying the grass-roots schemes for buying books that usually run in schools – but instead allow the agents to order over the net and the points to accrue to the school. Anyone who knows children knows it is this mixture of public spiritedness and consumerism that appeals to them.

Parents being encouraged to sign up with credit cards that will double the points that their children receive. In return for which the business is able to track the parent as well. Linking purchases in stores running the scheme with the parent and child.

You should try sending out mailings of suggested products for the e-kids' birthday or Christmas. Not lists full of guesses. Personalized lists that are compiled by a combination of what the e-kid has been looking at on site, TV, and in store. Lists that include what the e-kid has on his 'Dear Santa' type lists held online. Lists that tie into what the child's school is studying so that curriculum and gifts match.

Try out pocket-money schemes that allow mum or dad to put e-kid's allowance online via a cheque or credit card or bank transfer. This doubles his loyalty points and allows him to buy anything on an approved kid-friendly list from secure stores. Parents can receive statements showing what has been spent and children can have an online 'account' that shows their balance and purchases.

You could be one of the first to offer a 'myschool.com' service. Parents' lives so often revolve around their children. Guilt and anxiety about doing the right thing certainly play a part in parenting. They don't feel informed. They don't have time. Communication between schools and home is often a challenge.

Services that tie in homework requirements, books, projects, key dates to remember, school results, rules, approved stores for the purchase of uniforms, sports equipment. Such services would be able to contribute to smooth administration and to school funds via sales commission.

PTA meetings minutes could be held online. There could be facilities for online tuition or even online counselling. In this way everyone is helped and certain brands are imbued with solidity and trustworthiness as part of a sponsored advertising rich scheme. They are perceived as being community minded. And that is invaluable. Building services that respond to genuine problems is good for your business and the e-customer.

If you want to build a profitable market for e-kid spending power:

- Encourage them to get their parents to buy.

- Figure out how to help them to gain their own purchasing power.

- Build brand loyalty for the future.

That is the motivation to educate each successive generation. Ideally you figure out how to make even the education profitable so that you are still in business when the kid really starts to spend.

They play but will they pay? The oldest of Generation Y are

emerging from their teens. The youngest will be born in December 2001. We are talking about a rapidly changing, varied and distinctive group. So early on in its development it hardly seems fair to group them together since sometimes their differences, related to age, appear to outweigh their similarities, based on generation.

This age group does not represent the majority of web purchasing. In fact it does not even spend as great a percentage of its available budget on the web as other groups. Perhaps it never will. Unless ...?

The value and interest in Generation Y should concentrate on at least four areas:

1 Invest now and reap loyalty later.

2 Use the web to affect purchases still made in the real world.

3 Understand the future of the e-customer from the behaviour of Generation Y.

4 Create services that invalidate the reasons why Generation Y still spends most of its money in the real world.

"Shops
on the net are not designed

A good look at Generation Y lifestyles reveals why they currently view shopping as a secondary reason for using the net.

First easy distinction to be made is: they are not adults. They do not have adult jobs or responsibilities. Most do not view the net as a way of 'achieving more' by 'doing less'. They are not thinking about how it can help them on the promotions ladder or save them money so they can balance the budget. Instead, they are thinking about how it can improve their social circle (sex and friends), their exam performance (revision and research), and pander to their curious fascination with the fad and the forbidden (diaryproject.com to see what they are thinking).

Shopping is not a chore for Generation Y – it is a chance to get away from their parents[33] and to hang out with their friends. They are also still novice consumers. They like to touch, try and compare products. They buy fashion items (clothes and electronics) that need to be seen and tried on before a final decision is made.

They also make group decisions and will show their friends what they are thinking of buying before handing over any money. This ensures acceptance by the group of the purchase. It also extends the pleasure of the purchase through the whole shopping trip. Window shopping turns into changing room shopping that eventually turns into the real thing.

Shops on the net are not designed to enhance the communal shopping experience. The net, designed by adults with hectic lifestyles, has tried to minimize the duration and interaction of the shopping experience.

enhance
the communal shopping exprience ,,

This is the case even where the design objective does not work and the shopping process is drawn out and inefficient.

This does not mean that shops should be overconfident about a future where teen shopping is safe from the ravages of the web. Old Father Time will turn these children and teens into adults with an aptitude for the web that will lead them increasingly to use it for purchases when time becomes a constraint. And before that happens, a bunch of businesses will start to remove the main obstacles to teen spendamania.

This will be done by halting your own body clock and prejudices and logging into the world of the e-teen and the net child. There's stuff out there that they value, websites that engage their attention.

There are some products that have sufficiently married Generation Y's lifestyle and aspirations with the available technology. Witness the birth of the fantastic Cybiko – a combination of an electronic organizer, a mobile phone, and a hand-held games machine all wrapped up in translucent colours. The whole company was set up to develop a 'Wireless Inter-tainment System'.

According to the Cybiko advert slogan: 'Change the way kids communicate, and you change the way they live'.

Having too much fun to shop?

The challenge for the service providers is that teens are benefiting from the 'free stuff' that is on the net designed to lure adults into buying and seeing advertising. The advertising still works in principle but the buying doesn't because there is very little in the proposed buying experience that meets the teen criteria for a fun and useful time.

The free stuff includes e-mail, research, games and chat rooms. All these take the average teen more time than it takes the average adult to undertake his more serious shopping tasks. He is hardly likely suddenly to leave the entertaining, fantasy world of his peers to pop into Wal-Mart to arrange a home delivery of sausages. It is improbable that he will leave the pleasures of an online game played against international competition to open an investment account. The web is just too good at meeting other needs and interests to be used lightly for boring, dull, adult activities.

Let's look for instance at the world of music. The web is 'awesome' for the e-teen music enthusiast who is likely to have scant regard for copyright. He can simply borrow tracks of CD quality recorded into the latest compact format (currently MP3) from an extended social circle many millions strong. He does not *have* to buy and the online purchasing experience has to work hard even to approach the fun of perusing such a vast music library.

Napster gets into their shoes because it offers them the chance to do

what they do already but much, much more easily. Since the invention
of the audio tape, teens have always swapped and copied music.
Compilations given to friends have upped credibility. Compilations
given to romantic interests have led to increased eye fluttering and
speeded up heart beats.

So organize a way for teens to swap music free from their computers,
connecting them to hundreds of thousands of tracks on thousands of
hard drives around the world. Then you have a hot product. Trouble is
that it took a teen to create the idea. And the teen didn't do it for money
so Napster has no plans to make a profit any time soon.

Once again it is easy to take the narrow view. Eminem, an outspoken
rap artist, certainly did when he recently gave his opinion (strongly
stated) that:

THE INTERNET IS TAKING

THE **WHOLE THRILL AWAY** FROM THAT ****.

IF YOU CAN AFFORD A **COMPUTER,**

YOU CAN **AFFORD TO PAY $16** FOR MY **** CD.

What he and many of the record companies forget is that they do
business in a world where one in ten or more CDs are counterfeit. Far
from threatening revenues, the advent of digital music actually provides
a way of avoiding the bootleg trade. Encrypted music and subscriber
internet channels for listening to new bands are both possibilities for
dealing profitably with the teen (music-loving) e-customer.

Online chat
The world of online chat is also an immensely entertaining medium
with precious little involvement from 'traditional' online manufacturers
and stores. Chat services were set up by an older generation in order to

"Take a stroll into the chat worlds of

yahoo.com, aol.com, or teenchat.com "

make money. It is not surprising that they do not recognize the importance of online teen communities.

Take a stroll into the chat worlds of yahoo.com, aol.com, or teenchat.com. There are adults here, but as a proportion of their age group teens are the represented the most.

Text chat is a way of carrying out a conversation by typing out what you want to say. You assume an identity (ideal for a teen seeking companionship) and start 'chatting' to a group on a particular subject. If you want to carry on a private conversation you can send a private message (PM) or start whispering. In this teen-friendly world you can carry on an infinite number of conversations without the group knowing. Whispering without anyone knowing? That's a killer feature.

Voice chat extends the power of instant messaging by adding public and private voice conversations via those multimedia computers that have headphones and microphones. Web cams add the further dimension of video to the proceedings.

Another evolution of all these forms of online, instant chat is the use of **avatars**. These are essentially little figurines or icons that you use to represent yourself as you chat (dobedo.com).[34] You can move your finger puppet around the screen and, as you type, the words come out of your character via cute little speech bubbles.

One, major step up from avatar chat is the introduction of three dimensions to create pithily titled **3D chat worlds** (www.palace.com). You assume not only an identity and an image but a complete body. You are free to explore, run about, move your arms, legs and head.

Often you can dance, jump, or even fly. It's rather like entering a computer game (like the Disney movie *TRON* or a low resolution version of MATRIX).

You could choose to exploit teen enthusiasm for such services by opening stores inside them. It's a virtual world with virtual locations. Why not integrate the two? That way the teen can shop and chat. He can also share his purchase. He can have home deliveries of food so that he can eat while he chats. He can compare and contrast. 3D offers the ideal way of demonstrating real-world objects. It can allow products to be spun around, clothes to be even tried on by modifying the avatar that is being used. It can even be used to add in objects to the experience by allowing them to be used as part of the game. Bikes, cars, phones could all have their virtual, branded equivalents. Virtual sales people or evangelists could be on hand to demonstrate and extol the virtues of their product. It's the ideal way to build up real-world buying impulses.

In becoming part of the e-teen world you will be able to experiment and find out what fits. It is far less likely that you will be able to drag e-teens along kicking because it is 'good for them' or lead them pied-piper like by simply using your idea of cool graphics.

Websites come from Mars

Most face-to-face e-customer service is delivered by women. Most commercial websites are designed by men. There is obvious potential here for a significant difference between the shopping experience priorities delivered by these two channels.

There is no point in being coy. Consider the average, normal, usual (perhaps stereotypical) experience when men and women shop together. And remember that if it is a stereotype, it is one that is enjoyed by hundreds of millions of couples worldwide.

This doesn't mean that men can't design for women. Or that women can't design for men. It does mean that in the normal course of things both need to accept that their personal shopping experience priorities are not shared by everyone. And particularly not by the opposite sex.

For a start there are some pretty major differences between the brains that male and female e-customers bring into their net encounters. As a indication of these divergences consider an extract from *Why Men Don't Listen and Women Can't Read Maps* by Allan and Barbara Pease:

WOMEN HAVE **SUPERIOR** COLOUR VISION, A **WIDER PERIPHERAL** VISION ... SPEAK ABOUT 20,000 WORDS PER DAY, **GET FRUSTRATED** IF THEY HAVE NOT SPOKEN **THEIR QUOTA**, AND VIEW SHOPPING **AS RELAXING.** MEN TEND TO FOCUS ON **ONE THING AT A TIME,** **WILL NOT SEE** THE BUTTER IN THE FRIDGE, ARE **COMFORTABLE** WITH ABOUT **7,000 WORDS** A DAY, AND REQUIRE **DEFINITIVE OBJECTIVES** FOR SHOPPING.[35]

Since the female e-customer can see things quickly (in the fridge or on screen) she will typically prefer many electronic, colour-coded options in one place so that she can find what she is looking for rapidly. The male e-customer may prefer to be led from one task to the next in a very compartmentalized way, relying on his spatial awareness to remember where to go to achieve his next goal.

The evidence suggests that men see asking for help as an indication of failure. So what do you do for a man who thinks this way? Provide as many self-help facilities as possible and offer to help in a positive way rather than forcing him to admit his need.

The female e-customer considers 'talking things through' as a desirable and necessary part of the shopping (or any other) experience. It may explain why so many still prefer to go into a shop and talk to a real person before making the final (already researched) purchase. So make sure you have a 'click to talk' facility on your website that allows real-time text or voice chat.

Are there any differences between the needs of male and female e-customers? Sure there are but they just might not be the differences that you might expect. There are subtleties and nuances. They often go against stereotypes, regardless of the direction of the perspective.

The top three sites in the US (amazon, cdnow and barnesandnoble) have broad-based appeal between male and female e-customers but after that major differences start to show.[36] So we find (big surprise) that women shop for stuff that affects them the most like health, beauty, clothing and toys. Men focus on entertaining themselves, booking travel for work (all those road warriors) and finding out about financial investments (keeping a roof over his family's head).

Consider the question of community. Some have argued that the net is the ideal tool for women to realize their natural need for building relationships. This may be true but it does not mean that they shop any less than men, which may not be a surprise to men holding other kinds of stereotypical opinions.

There are still some variations. The female e-customer tends to buy more basic items but she also tends to spend up to four times more on each purchase.

But men and women buy at the same times, about 50% after 5 pm and 20% after 8 pm, and they have the same worries about security, with approximately 80% considering it a pivotal issue, but they become less sensitive to these concerns as they grow older. They buy almost everything in identical patterns with the exception of computer purchases.[37]

Know your female e-customer

The female e-customer has not been slow in figuring out that the internet offers lots of the key benefits that she has previously enjoyed through catalogue shopping. They are both forms of home shopping, they both save time and allow shopping out of hours.[38]

The possibility of electronic channels is that they will appeal to women who also want benefits that are not often associated with catalogues, such as 'value for money' and 'shopping experience'. Once they are there, over one in three find it excellent in terms of convenience and ease of shopping. But too many have still not tried the route and need to be tempted in so that they can discover how sweet the fruit really is.

If you want to keep women clicking on your adverts and flocking to your site then you will need innovation on your side. The female e-customer loves 'new' even more than she likes 'free'.

A pretty amazing gender-based difference can be seen in the way that male and female e-customers respond to banner advertisements.[39] The female e-customer is more likely to click, more motivated by curiosity, less influenced by familiarity, more interested in new stuff. She loves animated adverts (70%) and hates pop-ups (8%).

"The female e-customer

loves 'new'

Don't be misled by statistics that forecast that women will be the largest group on the internet in a couple of years. These figures are extrapolations of web growth rates that are high mainly because they are catching up with the men! This statistic will be replaced with the next fastest growing group until all groups have reached saturation.

It is more notable to find that the internet is approaching the status of lipstick or the ubiquitous handbag, with 70–85% of female e-customers saying that they 'cannot imagine life without it'.[40]

What you should care about is that the female e-customer controls almost 80% of all purchasing decisions for her household. Even when she doesn't buy online you can be pretty sure that she has already used the net to inform her decision (96% of the time).

So when she demands 'fast and easy solutions' you had better listen. Don't keep trying to lure her in with bargains. She wants a simpler life (83%) more than she wants to save money (55%).[41] Security concerns will stop her buying (40%)[42] but price won't.

Women like sport! More than one in three that go online spend some time retrieving sports news from the internet, so it makes sense to include sports headlines on any site, even if it is directed mainly at female e-customers (women.com and ivillage.com).[43]

As she uses the net for shopping she abandons other channels (retail and catalogue) but many (40%) still revert to the real world to make the final transaction. She doesn't enjoy or trust the shopping experience enough to follow it through to the final submit button.

even more than she
likes 'free' ”

The challenge is to convince women to take the first steps into the virtual world. And that has got to happen through advertising that actually demonstrates how the services are used. It will also be vital to ensure that women experience the electronic world when they are enjoying their real-world shopping experience.

Remember the local difference lessons because much of the current evidence is based on surveys conducted in the US. This is often contradicted by experiences in other parts of the world. For example, in complete contrast to the US, in Japan more women go online for entertainment than for business.[44]

So to attract men and women it will make sense to have a mixed team of managers, designers, usability experts, programmers, content providers and testers. That is how you will ensure that the needs of both groups are met and that you maximize the benefits to you of the difference between them.

Solving mothers' dilemmas

YOU TAKE IT **ALL OFF THE SHELVES.** YOU PUT IT ALL IN THE **TROLLEY.** YOU TAKE IT ALL TO THE **CHECKOUT.** YOU PUT IT ALL ON THE **CONVEYOR BELT.** YOU PUT IT ALL BACK **INTO THE BAGS.** YOU PUT ALL THE **BAGS BACK INTO THE TROLLEY.** YOU TAKE IT ALL **TO THE CAR.** YOU PUT ALL THE BAGS IN THE **CAR.** YOU DRIVE IT ALL BACK **HOME.** YOU TAKE IT ALL **OUT OF THE CAR.** YOU **UNLOAD** ALL THE BAGS. YOU PUT IT ALL ON THE **SHELVES AT HOME.**
IN OUT IN OUT.

A mother's work, it is said, is never done. That is a fantastic opportunity to meet the 'do less, achieve more' motivations that are common to so many purchases of technology. What's more, you have an advocate, or many, at home waiting to support your nifty, new, time-saving stuff. The family will be full of ideas. Any excuse to justify a new computer with the excuse of a helpful service for Mom.

So what does Mum actually do that might need the help of the internet in its various guises? What could a set of interconnected computers, systems and databases do for her in her day-to-day life that would convince her to become a convert?

Just to start with, you have three distinct mother groups:

- The mother who uses computers for some parts of her life, perhaps at work or to write a letter, but is undecided – the **mayb-e-mum**.

- The mother who dislikes and distrusts the world of electronics – the **anti-e-mum**.

- The **e-mum** – wired from the oven to the kindergarten.

And there are so many ways to help them all. We want them all as profitable e-customers but we have to decide where to start. So we will focus on the two extremes of e-mum and anti-e-mum.

Anti-e-mum

Anti-e-mum has adopted a negative stance towards computers for one of a number of reasons. Understanding the reasons are important if you are to discover ways of unlocking her potential as a valuable e-customer.

She may have decided that computers are bad. That they steal away the children and her husband. That they let you down when you most need them. That they intrude unpleasantly into her pleasant and aesthetically pleasing home. That they have replaced people. That they are rude and prying. She may have seen *The Net*, *2001* and *The*

Terminator and a dozen other movies where the machine is the villain.

She likes pens, paper, multicoloured post-its, and books. She did not like *Star Wars*. She has never played a computer game (unless forced to by a child or her husband). She uses a mobile phone because they are convenient but she cannot bring herself to program in any telephone numbers.

> " The anti-e-mum **represents a challenge** because she does **not want** to be converted "

The anti-e-mum represents a challenge because she does not want to be converted. An admittedly religious analogy, but accepting new ways of doing things is certainly linked to our life perspective. However, there is a way!

Just bear in mind the limitations in her mind and create solutions where the technology is invisible. She does not like it *so hide it*. Background computing is the way of the future for many users. The anti-e-mum is just a very extreme example. She will never be impressed with the details, only with the results. She will be demanding not because she understands what you are doing but precisely because she has no idea.

Matching her needs to background computing is the key. Find ways to help record her children's lives by doing cute things with video, photographs and audio. Assist her in educating her children and reach out to make her meet her own life's goals.

Services like these can be made profitable in their own right by attracting advertising or direct subscription. They are also valuable components that can be incorporated into much less interesting service offerings. Dull insurance products online can certainly become more relevant if they are linked to how she feels about her family.

To some extent such services already exist (myfamily.com). The challenge is to make them easier and more convenient. To disguise them and at the same time bring their advantages to the attention of the anti-e-mum by ensuring that the message is presented in the media (or by people) that she does trust.

E-mum

Now we turn our attention to that keen enthusiast of technology – e-mum. The art is not to hide the technology but find ways of using what she has already purchased to lock her into buying your stuff.

What might she have already in her e-mum handbag, rucksack or desk? There is a mobile phone, a personal digital assistant and at least one home computer. Quite apart from the potential for family computers both in and out of the immediate home, there will also be computers in the outside world – school, shops, doctors, offices – that hold data or services that she uses.

We need to provide services that connect this network together to make life easier, flashier or more fun. You need to figure out what she is already doing and which services she is using so that you can add your service to what she already likes as a value-added bonus. The e-mum likes to use the technology so she wants to find things that are new. Fun stuff. She enjoys it. You need to ask yourself whether your service or product gives her that techno-buzz.

But that is only the start. The next step is to sustain interest because the e-mum has no problem trying out something new and then abandoning it because it doesn't impress her.

Don't call me grandpa

Getting older. Fantastic fun but not great if you like to be treated as an individual rather than an age group. The 'silver surfer' moniker has been attributed to those older than 50 by the traditional media to neatly combine greying hair and web activity. But, as any marvel.com knows, the original silver surfer was a comic book anti-hero. He stood strong, metallic and proud, riding around the world on a mystical surfboard.

His oft repeated cry, 'I hold the power cosmic, I am invincible' seems pretty appropriate for a group that wields immense influence, buying power, and is using electronic channels to relaunch themselves and their needs on the virtual world.

They make no excuses and are just as deadly as the 20-something when the weapon of choice is a keyboard. Listen to one such grumpy declaration of independence from webcurmudgeon.com.

SO HERE YOU GO. GRAMPS IS HERE TO SHOW YOU THAT YOUNG, PURPLE-HAIRED, NOSE-RINGED WEB PUNKS **ARE NO MATCH FOR OLD AGE,** METAMUCIL AND DENTURES. **I HOPE YOU LIKE IT,** IF NOT, YOU **CAN GO SUCK EGGS!**

Do the majority of entrepreneurs suffer from gerontophobia? What else but a 'morbid, irrational fear of, or aversion to old people or growing old' would explain the style of advertising, websites and electronic services focused on them?

The silver haired e-customer is 30% less likely to jump hastily into a spontaneous purchase than those aged under 25,[45] and tends to stay with a group of favourite sites that is 25% smaller. Growing older has

" stop trying to use advertising that is only aimed at one age group "

the virtue of teaching patience and the pleasures of established tastes. So stop bugging him with insolent young pop-up adverts.

And stop trying to use advertising that is only aimed at one age group. The recent set of advertisements for thestreet.com, US investor portal, are illustrative. They confuse being off colour with being witty. Someone must have told them that advertising about drooping 38-inch Double Ds and erectile dysfunction would be universally appealing. Who do they think is doing all the investment?

Others attempt to 'humanize' their electronic channels with pictures of the young sending out a not too subtle message about what kind of e-customer is welcome. And it happens because older people at the top of organizations are afraid of not being up to date so they hand over marketing to younger people who sometimes only really reflect their own interests or their clichéd view of the interests of other people.

The issue of music online provides a good illustration of how different the attitudes and preferences of young and old e-customers can be.

Oldie.com makes sure that the old and useful do not stay old and discarded. It works with artists to re-record their greatest hits so that they can offer them to e-customers on the net. Then it allows e-customers to build up a custom CD from the music library and have it on its way to you within 24 hours. How cool is that?

So everyone is happy (except the original record company and that's not the e-customer's problem). It's the message of electronic channels. E-customers and the stuff they like do not reduce in value just because they have grown older. In fact the opposite is usually true.

Older e-customers are ideal candidates for legal net music because they have consciences that are bothered by the apparently illegal copying of music via tools from sites such as Napster.com and gnutella.com.[46]

Fifty-year-old writer and musician Steve Bass from Pasadena, California uses the Internet to download jazz tunes using Napster:

MORALLY I'VE GOT TO STOP,

I'VE GOT A REAL CONFLICT CONCERNING THE

USE OF THE SOFTWARE.

Know your older e-customer

There is a very attractive agelessness on the web where no one can patronize your wrinkles. But sometimes this is achieved through becoming invisible rather than by benefiting from age equality in the virtual world. The downside to anonymity comes when equality is just the by-product of depersonalization.

Failing to treat the older e-customer as an individual means that the service can fail to adapt to his particular needs and interests. Perhaps he would prefer to have the text on the screen a little larger. He might like to speak to someone rather than continue to point and click through tired hands.

It's a group who share certain frugal sensibilities honed by recessions, depressions and rationing. Some have the inclination and the time to use money-saving services like lowermybills.com that allows consumers to research ways to reduce many types of monthly bills, including credit cards, utilities, insurance and internet services bills.

No silly Generation X advertising here then. How about something with a little more class, a little more nostalgia, and a lot more respect? Call on older advertising executives, past masters, and ask them to create new classics. It's true everywhere, but electronic channels allow more choices and can support many more extremes differences than any supermarket ever could.

Since interest and aptitude in the virtual world are not dependent wholly on physical capability or age, it would be wrong to make too many assumptions. Who will really spend all day online? The rushed-off-his-feet 35-year-old or the retired, relaxed 65-year-old? This is going to lead to some generational blushes as parents and grandparents get wired before their progeny:

AN EMBARRASSING SITUATION.

MY MOTHER IS NOW USING HOMERUNS.COM ONLINE GROCERY SERVICE, AND **I AM STILL VISITING STORES.** I'VE GOT TO GET THE WEBSITE COMPLETED AND GET THIS STUDY FORMALLY UNDERWAY. **MY MOTHER** (I.E., MS LOW-TECH): HAS CABLE, FAX, AND **IS LIVING** IN THE **INTERNET AGE** BY **SHOPPING** FOR HER GROCERIES **ONLINE.** ME (I.E., COMPUTER SCIENCE DEGREE, WORKED IN HIGH-TECH, PHD FROM MIT): **NO CABLE,** NO FAX, STILL **LIVING IN THE DARK AGES** BY VISITING BRICKS AND MORTAR RETAIL STORES.

This example, from the 24/7 internet project (people.bu.edu/celtics/index.html), illustrates a fairly common situation. An older generation is underestimated. It can type the word, see the screen and pay the bills. And on the whole that's all you need to qualify as prime e-customer material. Still think you can't teach an old mouse new clicks? Think again.

The enabled disabled

In principle, electronic channels should help to create an equal access culture for those with different abilities. The money-making principle should encourage business to focus on the needs of over 10% of the population. And the 'let's not get sued' principle should be enough to motivate the 'abled' to reach out to the 'disabled'.

Let's try the stick first just in case someone out there doesn't get it. In most of the existing internet universe it is illegal not to provide equal access for all. The US was one of the first to legislate to improve accessibility with the Disabilities Act of 1990 which states:

ALL NEWLY CONSTRUCTED PLACES OF **PUBLIC ACCOMMODATION** AND COMMERCIAL FACILITIES **MUST BE ACCESSIBLE** TO INDIVIDUALS WITH DISABILITIES TO THE EXTENT THAT IT IS NOT **STRUCTURALLY IMPRACTICABLE..**

The virtual world has been included within the remit of this law. It has been successfully argued that it is a public space that should be subject to the same demands as any other area.

In support of the spirit and letter of the law, the organizations that are responsible for agreeing standards on the internet have worked together on the specifications of the latest version of HTML (the core internet language) to make it universally accessible.

Using the new standard allows little bits of information to be included that permit web pages to be more easily interpreted by a variety of non-standard browsers. It also allows devices like screen readers, which take code intended for a monitor and send it to a speech synthesizer or a refreshable Braille display.

Elsewhere the web accessibility initiative (WAI) has continued to publish guidelines that can dramatically improve the usefulness of the internet to those with aural, visual or motor impairment.[47] At wai.com it is possible to read the standards and have your site accredited.

Don't make excuses. It's easy to find out whether a site is compliant. There are even automated tools like 'bobby' that allow businesses simply to type in the address of the web page in question and have it analyzed for any area of weakness. If the site passes it is entitled to proudly display its Bobby Approved icon.

It has to be the most enlightened approach for making more profits and the world a better place. A point well made by Gary Presley speaking about general levels of accessibility on a micro site about disability issues within about.com:

A SMART BUSINESS PERSON SHOULD APPRECIATE THAT.
A SMART BUSINESS PERSON, IN FACT, **SHOULD BE EAGER** TO TAKE VOLUNTARY
ACTION TO IMPROVE **ACCESS FOR CUSTOMERS.** IF HE'S SMART ENOUGH,
YOU WON'T HAVE TO BELABOUR THAT POINT.
ANYONE WHO **ISN'T HANDICAPPED** BY THE **LACK OF**
COMMON SENSE SHOULD RECOGNIZE
A LACK OF **ACCESSIBILITY**
REDUCES BUSINESS TRAFFIC AND SALES.

That is what a smart business person would do. Don't you agree? Fortunately, extending access to those without internet access is catching on. Businesses have realized that e-customers with home PC web access are only one small part of a

"Doing difficult stuff

that your e-customers

want is the source of

competitive advantage"

networked world. If a business can attract just a small proportion of the billions of telephone users then it is on to a good thing.

Just think about the benefits. An immediate increase in potential e-customers. Its also a way of doing something that your competitors are not doing. It's not simple and that is even better. Doing difficult stuff that your e-customers want is the source of competitive advantage.

E-customers with visual impairment still want to reduce the cost of long-distance telephone bills and search for valuable information. New services from priceline.com and lycos.com will benefit from this group's business since the services are provided via speech recognition that communicates with the same systems that support their websites.

As the fight for the mass market becomes fierce it is in the niches that new riches will be uncovered. So concluded a recent television competition broadcast by channel4.co.uk to find the UK's best dot-com idea. After sifting through 7,000 entries, £1 million in venture capital was awarded funding to youreable.com, the brainchild of Joe Rajko.

Finding profitable new e-customer groups should be high on the list of priorities for every business, so they should naturally focus on the lucrative possibilities of the disabled. If they don't try to create reasonable levels of access they will be penalized legally. If they don't get more creative than that then they are missing the point and the potential profits of enabling the disabled.

The hunt

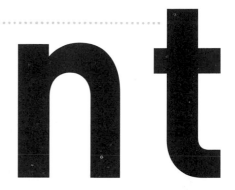

" Don't minimize the differences "

Mind grab

So you want to grab my attention as an e-customer? Makes sense. It's certainly the only way to take your share of my money.

You have a whole lot of competition and numerous options. The combination of different ways of attracting e-customers to your site is complex. It requires an understanding of the possibilities and their usage patterns.

You're right. Advertising has been reinvigorated by the profileration of media channels. Electronic media has inspired new ways of achieving the age-old commercial aims of attracting e-customers to look at what you are selling and stay around long enough to buy and then buy again.

Imagine your electronic offering surrounded by a series of concentric circles. Way out there beyond the furthest edge of the outermost circle are those who know nothing about your wonderful stuff. Loyal, repeat buying e-customers are at its centre.

The e-customer dislikes advertising. He values the internet for being sales-pressure free. So if you are too blatant he will be chased away. The majority who still do not purchase online will be put off trying. Maybe not forever but your offering will be last on his list.

No one likes being hassled

If he is particularly smart and has a strong antipathy for advertising the e-customer may already have adopted one of the several products that simply cut out the ads. A product like the one from AdSubtract.com that will block unwanted advertisements and fend off electronic tags (cookies). As each is removed it is accompanied by the rousing sound of machine gun fire filling e-customers like Tiff with gratitude:

I ABSOLUTELY LOVE THIS SERVICE! YOU HAVE NO IDEA!

WELL, MAYBE YOU DO BUT I **JUST HAD TO SAY** YOURS IS

THE BEST IDEA I'VE SEEN

SINCE BEING ON THE WEB OVER THREE YEARS AGO.

TODAY I'VE **SAVED MYSELF** OVER 400 ADS AND 10 COOKIES.

THANK YOU!!!!!!!!!!!!

I'M SPREADIN' THE WORD.

To avoid being shot repeatedly you will need to make the stuff so much fun that the e-customer feels he has received more than enough back for his attention. In fact he probably doesn't view it as advertising or marketing at all. Just as children don't question the motives of whoever puts the toys in cereal boxes. It's just viewed as a bonus, a benefit.

This growing immunity or antipathy among e-customers to advertising means that the focus needs to shift from straight 'come and get it' advertising to content-based 'you'll like these' marketing.

Collectables are high on the list when it comes to this enlightened brand-building approach. It's more effective to create electronic stuff that everyone wants that boosts your brand awareness among e-customers. It costs very little to distribute and it creates a strong bond. The e-customer is being taught that he should be seeking out the brand because it can offer him something. Far better than him feeling that he is being actively hunted.

Take a look, for example, at 'Things' – collectable interactive multimedia files, created by Steve Barlow and Eric Bedell, and their business ThingWorld.com. Copyrighted and tamper proof, the business supplies digital, interactive baseball cards that can be collected by the fans. All 'Things' link directly to the relevant website, driving traffic and increasing brand awareness. So, for example:

FOR WWF **FANS** THERE IS A FULL SET INCLUDING ONE THE **RATTLESNAKE** THING DEDICATED TO **STONE COLD** STEVE AUSTIN COMPLETE WITH AN ANIMATED RATTLESNAKE **WAGGING ITS TAIL,** THE WRESTLERS THEME AND PHOTO. OR THE WILL SMITH THING THAT ALLOWS THE E-CUSTOMER TO **MIX HIS OWN VERSION** OF ONE OF THE STAR'S HIT TRACKS.

Banner advertising

Despite its prevalence, the **banner** is starting to show its age as the oldest of all new media advertising forms. It's a mixture between the hoardings placed around sports venues, off-the-page advertising positioned around articles, and those billboards that change message every so often. It is usually positioned in the same place on every page within a website.

It has significant differences that mark it out from its direct advertising forebears. A banner can be animated to show different messages as it is watched. This can attract attention. It can also deliver the rest of the message or punchline in what is usually limited space.

It can be used to build up general brand awareness, but inherent in the banner model is the call to action. The call to click. In this sense it includes the 'call this number now' free phone concept. And wrapped up in its little bundle is the ability to know how many people have seen it, how many have clicked on it and which sites attracted visitors. This kind of knowledge can be used to direct the banner clicking e-customer to the part of the page that is relevant to his interest.

This is potentially disturbing for the smoke and mirrors ad man. Those who are happy to stand by the effectiveness measure of advertising will love it. The creative leap is still as valid as ever. But the belief that we never know which half of the advertising works is becoming less true. Except for real twists it will be possible to know which online ads have been seen and in which order to lead the e-customer to the final sale.

Random advertising messages from third parties can have a damaging effect. The carefully crafted aesthetic is ruined (see Disney.co.uk). The e-customer is given a very strong message about the ease with which his attention is being sold by the company he originally wanted to know more about. Only little sites can afford to accept big banners.

The bigger you are, and the bigger you intend becoming, the more you need to avoid 'in your face' advertising messages. Check out the itty, bitty banner ads on yahoo.com. You still see the advert but it is hard to resent it.

> ## " Random advertising messages from third parties can have a damaging effect "

Interstitial advertising

As the banner ad becomes part of the background for the e-customer, advertisers fear that it will cease to be either irksome or compelling. Noting the link between irritating and noticeable, the **interstitial advert** was born.

It seeks to have more in common with the television ad in that it cannot be easily avoided. Its potential downfall is that it becomes like those magazine inserts that get in the way of what you are trying to do.

Any brand on the insert or the interstitial becomes associated with blocking the e-customer's aspirations.

It pops up when you move from one page to another and has to be explicitly discarded. The window it is in has to be consciously closed. Just bear in mind that if you come into my space you had better have something worthwhile to say.

The huge mistake made by autobytel.com illustrates the point. It tries very hard to be useful by including a competition, a free online mechanic service, and an online newsletter in its interstitial invitation. All the e-customer has to do is fill in his details. But the advert pops up on every visit and never takes the hint that the e-customer is not interested. It loses points in the fight because it behaves like the worst cars salesperson in the real world.

Advertising can be ineffective

The rebirth of real-world advertising has been much hyped. Try lots of excess cash, marketing inexperience and large egos rather than proven effectiveness in boosting virtual world brands. Not surprising that so many dot.coms have been fleeced by old media when one considers the sheep-like attitude they have demonstrated towards methods of getting the brand known.

The advice tends to be given that it is only possible to win if the brand is widely advertised. The funds flowed in from investors anxious to benefit from a revolutionary wave of commerce. With money and motive both present, the result was a stream of largely ineffective and very expensive advertising.

Often the web address is not even shown. So how is the e-customer meant to find his way to the site? It is unrealistic to expect them all to want the service or product so much that they will all search for the name until they find it.

Awareness of the net has risen. But not the specific brands. Not the specific benefits of the advertised service. Not even the advantages that the e-channels can bring to the e-customer. There has been a lot of flag waving and very little education or selling.

So now the e-customer knows that he is dealing with services offered by the new kid millionaires. He knows that the services start with www. And he knows that they all have weird names and whirly symbols in their logos.

Can't think of a worst start for a new channel. Yet despite this, usage continues to grow because once you realize how good it is you are hooked.

Over-advertising has been prevalent. High-profile events have been used. The Superbowl has been particularly popular in the US. Sponsorship of leading TV programmes, stunning (loss-leading) deals advertising on prime (expensive) time TV have been employed.

The results of over-advertising are usually negative. It overstretches the systems that provide the service. It creates peaks of demand that cannot be dealt with by the infrastructure that has been put in place. Or it demands infrastructures that are more highly specified (costly) than they needed to be.

E-customers rush towards the promised land only to find its borders closed or that they are in a queue that stretches back to Egypt. They do not like to wait. They stop waiting. They lose the trust that your loss-leading campaign was relying upon to increase selling via relationship selling.

Over-advertising also places unfair demands on staff that lead, in turn, to poor morale and its bedfellows: inferior service and staff unrest. Both cost the business dearly. Both compromise the business case which is almost universally based on repeat sales and market share over the long term.

It is no good relying on repeat sales that are based on unproven loyalty, non-existent systems and strategic wishful thinking. Relationships require a long time to develop. They require time to get them right. They tend to develop best where growth is predictable and long term.

Relationship campaigns are needed that are gradual, incremental, that understand the nature of a relationship. Not a quick win of a customer relationship management programme: the marketing catch-all.

You have to build a relationship. A one-night stand takes approximately one night. Courting takes a little longer. Why would building a commercial relationship be any different? You want to gain the potential customer's trust. Get inside their inner circle. Be accepted and looked to for answers. And through them to reach out to their immediate family, extended family, close friends and associates.

It's more about the grass roots. Rarely does a relationship of trust appear overnight. The companies we believe in have typically been around for years – those that have grown organically. They have justified themselves over a long time. Now sometimes we accept them as a default. But repeat sales are more likely with those we have known for a while.

You can't simply get around it by insisting that you are a friend after all. To speed it up you need to understand the actions that develop such relationships and increase the cycle of relationship building.

Even in the internet world, the leading, profitable brands like Yahoo! have been around long enough for their e-customers to reminisce about the 'good old days'. They have grown up with their e-customers and have learnt the craft of being a portal.

It has become a more than useless cliché that internet success requires mega old-world advertising. Typical of this was the entrepreneur who explained to me that he felt it was necessary to have $30 million available to support his dream project with TV advertising. In his view it was sensible to wait three years to gather funds before commencing the project.

Major error of judgement. There are good reasons for waiting but *don't* wait for advertising. A valuable e-customer brand *can* and should be built up from the grass roots. It is a networking thing and it needs communities and the connected if it is to be self-supporting.

billboard

"A valuable e-customer brand can and should be built up from the grass roots"

Recommendation – a powerful form of advertising

Far more effective than TV advertising of electronic channels is the **advertorial** – the well-placed discussion of your service by trusted programmes broadcast to those who are interested enough to watch. Or the clever service placement in TV drama, comedy or soap opera. The e-customer will be more likely to copy if he sees favourite characters from TV and film using the service. Seeing Joey from *Friends* using kozmo.com to deliver popcorn so he can watch the football uninterrupted will do more for such services than any amount of advertising.

Or any form of recommendation. If your service is worth using, tell a few e-customers about it and get them working on your behalf: evangelists. Link in a rewards scheme (beenz.com). Include the ability to e-mail interesting information and stuff to friends (zdnet.com). Bed down your service in the networks of trust operated by the e-customer and your service will grow healthy, long-term roots.

Mistrust anyone who argues otherwise. Wingspanbank.com spent over $100 million on advertising for fewer than 50K customers. X.com spent nothing on advertising and focused on how to build recommendation into the service itself. It allows an e-customer to send 'money' via e-mail but the recipient has to register in order to receive it. A two for one policy that has racked up over 3 million e-customers so far.

Also consider **billboard advertising** as a way of encouraging those in the real world. As long as a clear benefit is sold, complete with web address or channel, the likely first port of call for the e-customer will be the advertised electronic destination.

advertising

Even better than this is advertising through appliances that are located by the sales mechanism. The location-based mobile phone 'wapvert', that knows you are in the house and prompts you with another service. It's so much easier to act on impulse if the opportunity to buy is made simple.

It becomes prompting rather than advertising, as each appliance in the home becomes more intelligent. Or as the mobile phone develops into something capable of recognizing context, location and preferences and coming up with best matches to all three. We will start to welcome the prompt rather than dread it.

Regardless of what method is used, the e-customer's viewpoint must be adopted. You gotta sell the benefits. You need to step into the e-customer's mind and create a vision, a patter, an image and a service that his mind is conditioned to accept.

Electronic channels amplify imagination and expertise. If there is nothing there to amplify, the result is very loud silence. Noise about nothing. Feedback. Distortion. And the e-customer wonders why he is listening to so much pointless static.

Whisper nonsense in a crowd and no one will realize what you are saying. Shout it down a loud-speaker system and the world will know that you are a fool. Earn respect and you will be surprised how far your voice carries.

The night has a thousand eyes

So you got the e-customer in your sights and on to your site. Well done. The guy is in your shop. Sitting in your office. Looking at your brochures. What are you going to do with him now?

Better question. Would you even know that he was looking? The e-customer can be tracked every step of the way. He can be identified. He can be herded. He can be branded, tagged and corralled.

Too often a business is simply not actively tracking the e-customer. It has no idea where he is or what he is doing. This is puzzling considering the money that it has cost to lure him and thousands of other e-customers here. It's money slipping through downsized, corporate fingers if you let him get away. It's like inviting people to a discussion group to learn more about their views, then getting up, leaving the room and leaving no tape recorder running.

Remember that interaction in the virtual world is not automatically visible. It takes place remotely inside a microchip and along optical cable. The e-customer can see one side of that transaction through his computer screen but there may be no human representative involved.

No one to check whether the e-customer is happy, whether they want anything else, or why they didn't buy. No one to step in when the process is getting in the way of doing business. No one to explain why it didn't work or apologize.

No one to stop the shoplifting or the street hawkers diverting e-customers from your door. Does this happen in ethical e-space? Sure does. And it's so easy to do.

On yahoo.com (the world's biggest portal website and the first major web media star), it was noticed that the chat link appeared to have been hijacked. In e-customers went to join a standard chat session – click went the mouse – instead of landing into chat, e-customers found themselves on another website's home page.[48]

Come on. You have to admit that it would seem attractive to divert all the e-customers that attempt to use chat on yahoo.com to your site. Your share of Yahoo!'s millions of e-customers. No advertising necessary. And it will probably be ignored by many users who assume that the confusion is accidental.

Would your business know if it happened to your website? And that's hardly the only shenanigans that could be going on. Any crime, con or craft that can be found in the real world can be found here. And it can be even easier to disguise. Often no real people are involved in the process so there is no one to act suspicious on your behalf.

Even if some of the crime was visible, just bear in mind that the number of people that opened the 'love bug' virus is proportionate to the number of people who would not have a clue what they were witnessing. You need crime prevention officers in place to stop others stealing from your e-customers and from stealing your e-customers away from you.

This invisibility also means that there is no automatically generated anecdotal evidence or first-person experience of e-customer problems. Everything could be going wrong and the first time a business would know about it is when the sales figures go through the floor.

How to track your e-customer
Now of course one solution to the problem is to add the human touch back into the electronic relationship or keep asking the e-customer for feedback. You could even also start using the system yourself as an e-customer.

But quite apart from those approaches, the electronic nature of the transactions offers its own solution to its invisibility to the human eye. Electronic interactions can allow the e-customer to be tracked, counted and analyzed more rapidly and more accurately than ever before.

❝❝Someone is out there

And even better, electronic tracking can allow widespread personalization of marketing and service to the e-customer.

Someone is out there hunting for the e-customer and they are probably using better weapons than you are. You want to drag him back to your cave to turn him into clothing and food. To achieve the value transformation you will need to know where he is, how he feeds, how to trap and how to preserve.

Some of the most effective shopping experiences seem to hypnotize. From the first sight of an attractive, unthreatening home page to the first return visit. Allowing each e-customer to go at his own pace while entertaining and informing at every step. Judicious use of colours and features to ensure that he is headed in the right direction.

If he gets there without being dragged or pushed it will always be marked out as his decision: something he wanted to do and therefore something that he might want to try again. After the first purchase has been made, the pace is still with the e-customer but the facilities can be positioned to suit the repeat purchaser.

Suggestions about future buying need to appear alongside what the e-customer is doing. Remove any complicated purchase process and go direct to one-click purchases. The hypnotic message is delivered, 'No effort. No effort and so many good things to buy'. The chant goes on and the happy e-customer keeps right on buying. Not all at once but gradually his buying behaviour will become habitual. Not irreversible but established as the default.

hunting for the e-customer and they are probably using better weapons than you are "

Plot your tracking data – every point, click, search and download – and you will see the footsteps and fingerprints of your e-customers. The steps, about-turns and lingering will become clear, like the worn-down steps of an ancient castle marking out favoured routes.

Hunters through the ages have looked for wildlife trails in the bush. Once you know what paths your quarry uses you can start thinking about that cook-out beneath the stars. It is possible to follow them or to prepare any number of traps.

It is best to consider the e-customer in his natural habitat. As any twitching birdwatcher or gorilla observing naturalist will tell you. You need to study the real e-customer doing the stuff that he really does in the life he really has. That is how you will build services that catch the e-customer.

Build up a multi-dimensional picture of the e-customer so he can be observed from different angles. Include all the places that the e-customer can be and all the characteristics he can have. His age, his country, his job, his family, his role.

Revolve him to understand his perspective and needs arising from different roles and locations. If you look hard enough for ways to help you will find opportunities away from the frenzy of start-ups, the cliché of socio-economics and the dangers of demographics.

Choice or segmentation

It may be tempting to rely on the standard demographical groups that have been the staple of marketing campaigns for so long. The theory is that business just needs to discover enough about an e-customer to find out which group he is part of and therefore what else he wants to buy.

They are often pretty crude groupings despite the sophistication of the modelling that produces them. Can you really serve an individual by depersonalizing him first? If it was ever possible it seems less and less likely as the twin forces of fragmentation and globalization sweep into town.

The mighty Claritas, the US-based research company, admits the trend. It reckons that the number of groups has grown 50% since the 1970s resulting in more than 62 distinctive lifestyles in the US by the start of 2000.

Fragmentation is creating more and more subgroups that do not neatly fit within historic economic or social strata. Globalization is reducing the impact of geography as a source of lifestyle difference. People are living as tribes with no physical proximity required, brought together as a result of global marketing, television, and the net itself. The bigger the group, the more cliques are formed.

Isn't it more likely that the methods for segmentation have simply become more sophisticated and have identified lifestyle groups within or across the previously identified groups? Do you really think that people were ever so similar that meeting their needs was as simple as choosing a segment and selling to them with advertising that strikes the desired chord?

It is more probable that the evolved customer has just tired of being treated as a statistical grouping. New technologies allow personalized choice. They allow the e-customer to make his own decisions about what he wants to wear, drive, and cuddle up to at night. He is uncomfortable with the process and is beginning to voice his concerns, as the following question from one UTNE reader demonstrates:

WILL **MORE AND MORE** DEEMING REDUCE INDIVIDUALS TO THE **EMPTY SPACE** INSIDE THE DATA THAT MAKES THEM **UNIQUE?** IF ABSOLUTE POWER **CORRUPTS ABSOLUTELY,** WHAT ABOUT **ABSOLUTE KNOWLEDGE?**

It may not be a fight to the death. There may be room in town for the both of them but there is undoubtedly a possible conflict between two different ways of delivering personalized products and services: choice or segmentation.

So it should be a simple choice. But even so there are still significant differences in our individual needs within the same segment or cluster of society.

Two people may be in the same grouping for age range, ethnic group, wealth band, style of housing and family structure but not share the same aspirations or value the same elements of service or product design. Stop judging and start thinking.

make th

Spin them 360 degrees and make them dizzy The

idea of being able to see everything seems very attractive to a species who naturally has such a limited view. The 360° question is certainly key to hunting the e-customer.

First of all you have the **360° e-customer**. Let's treat him as a whole. Let's consider all aspects, '360 degrees', of the relationship. If you get this right you have literally every angle covered. There are no more sharp-pointed problem areas where the e-customer is left unsupported. Instead he fits into a neat circle of consideration. Wherever he tries to get out, he finds a soft curve of comfort, and problem resolution.

The company becomes the e-customer's number one fan. And we should all remember what happened to Paul Sheldon in the film of the Steven King book *Misery*. As a reminder, the author is involved in an accident. He is found and then shackled to the bed. And just in case he ever thinks of leaving his loyal fan, she breaks his ankles with a sledge hammer.

Apart from being a neat literary reference, it's a valuable warning about the dangers of this approach.

From this concept often comes the **360° e-customer contact** via what seems like 360 e-mails a day. I get them. You get them. More than 4 trillion of them are sent every year.[49] What is the difference for e-customers between efforts to 'keep them in touch' and 'making them dizzy'?

em dizzy

The answer should be usefulness and appropriateness. You are trying to become a friend. Part of a shortlist of trusted suppliers of whatever stuff it is that you supply. You want to join the inner circle. When a friend calls, I have time for him. The closer the friend, the more time I have. My time is not limitless though and so I judge the usefulness of the call. If time starts to drag, he tells me what I already know or, worse, repeats what he has already told me then the pleasure of the contact is diminished. I start to consider whether to limit the time I spend before I make my polite excuses and leave the conversation.

Even if it is useful, it must be appropriate. Even if it is appropriate, it must be interesting to me! These three tests must all be met if I am to keep a pool of goodwill open. He can make an occasional error but such errors eat away at the relationship.

66 If you send an e-mail

The e-customer dislikes it when a 'good' friend corners him to try and sell something at a party. Everyone dislikes it when the introductory 'how are you?' is immediately followed up by 'would you like to save money on ...'. But this is allowable if the product introduced is useful and the approach is not pushy.

What the e-customer hates is when that same 'good' friend (now living on his reserve pool of goodwill) brings up the same line, and products, after the same perfunctory pleasantries every time their paths cross.

So if you send an e-mail to an e-customer, make it useful, appropriate and interesting. Everyone hates junk e-mail but few people object to receiving useful, interesting and appropriate information and services.

360° e-mail

360° e-mail categories include: the 'something you can send to your family' e-mail; the 'this is something cool that I know you are going to like to do with our product' e-mail; the 'your friend has recommended you (and will be paid if you reply)' e-mail and 'your friend has prepared this for you' e-mail.

Unfortunately Spam (unwanted e-mail) is not so popular. It doesn't get read and if an e-customer notices your company name along with the rest he will link it with the unwanted as he hits the delete key and sends to the waste bin. Not a helpful connotation.

The challenge is to ensure that you have as many e-mails as possible with permission to use them. In this way you avoid your marketing campaigns being ruined by future legalities. You also increase ten fold

o an e-customer,

make it useful,

appropriate and interesting **" "**

the chances of the e-customer viewing the e-mail as a positive underlining of the relationship rather than as an unwanted intrusion.

Stars in the 360° e-mail firmament include realplayer.com and flash.com who between them attract more than 20 million unique e-customers a month. Not surprising because they use such a beguiling mix of usefulness and fun.

The Britney Spears e-mail sent out by realplayer.com deserved an electronic Grammy. In less than 100 words it managed to combine announcing a new version of its software and an attention-grabbing story about Britney's new single by providing the opportunity for e-customers to listen to it online using its software.

The e-customer lucky enough to be on the flash.com mailing list has enjoyed cartoons, games, music and competitions. All guaranteed to brighten your day in glorious, colourful contrast to the all text efforts of other e-mailing businesses.

The flash.com e-mails are so good that the e-customer will tend (and is invited) to pass them on to his friends. Often referred to as 'viral marketing' the idea is that the message you wish to push out to the e-customer becomes passed on from one e-customer to the next via e-mail. It's a kind of sophisticated sneezing.

Be careful to avoid your marketing efforts becoming associated with general viruses or intrusive, problematic e-mails. Hoax e-mails have already embarrassed businesses by offering free gifts. Asking people to pass along your very important electronic offer is not so very different from chain mails. You and the e-customer may lose friends together if he passes along your e-mail.

The term viral marketing may not be helpful. It describes either chain e-mails or recommendations passed along for a friend to see. Recommendations are the most helpful form and a better way of making your objectives clear. And they are about relationship building rather than infecting the recipient.

Also be wary about what kind of information to entrust to e-mail. Don't send out confidential stuff in an insecure message. Make sure that you get permission to send out the e-mails and don't buy other e-mail lists from other businesses. As the number of electronic communications we receive increases we will find patience only for those who seek our permission before sending and those who deliver useful content in a timely and unobtrusive manner.

Save your efforts for creating and sending e-customers stuff that helps and entertains them. Just let them know that it is there and they will start to use it. Save your electronic mail for those who really want to read it.

THE
EXPERIENCE

" For eight hours a day

I deal with indecisive yuppies, and

brain-dead bozos for chump change.

And you want me to smile? "

Ups and downs of the e-customer

You need to get into the peaks and troughs of the e-customer experience. The e-customer enters your site or channel on a high, full of expectations. That is why he is there. He may also be nervous. He may be in a hurry. It's a potentially fragile mix. He is willing to believe but demanding the very best.

From this point, where are you going to take him? He wants immediate attention. Your web pages or channel had better deliver soon. He wants to have his eyes pleased by what unfolds in front of them. He will always want more so it is very easy to disappoint.

You need to pitch key features. First, in the marketing. Then, in the advertising. When they arrive at your channel, site or store, **Step one** must let them know that they are in the right place. **Step two** must be recognizable in explaining why they chose to come. **Step three** must convince them that they were right to be fooled by the pitch.

You cannot afford to have them arrive on your site and leave them questioning why they bothered. Discover the different reasons why the e-customer has made the effort to find you. They either clicked or typed your name. It was a choice. Rarely a complete accident. Let them know that it wasn't a mistake.

As soon as the e-customer has arrived he is looking for where to go next. He needs to be made to feel at home. In this way he can start to achieve his aims in the visit. It helps if you know where he has come from and can make a good guess at figuring out what he wants before he asks.

Remember that the channel is there to solve problems. The design of the service has to help him to figure out whether you are the right place to help him. That doesn't mean something for everyone. Not

"Don't hide behind
introductory animations"

every site can or should be broad based. It does mean that you had better make it VERY CLEAR what you do and how that might meet his needs.

Don't hide behind introductory animations. Get rid of all the clutter. You are meant to be helping the e-customer to unclutter his life so make a start with the shopping experience. Make sure that he can move directly into meeting his needs at his own pace. Get to the point!

Kozmo.com gets straight to the point. It uses only 15 words to let the e-customer know what it can do for him and how to request the service. Here are all 15 words:

FREE DELIVERY TO YOU

IN LESS THAN AN HOUR.

WHERE DO YOU WANT YOUR DELIVERY?

Could it really be much more simple? If you said 'yes' then you have a real chance of meeting e-customer needs. You must exploit the medium and put all the other stuff elsewhere. Remove it from the critical path that flows between the e-customer and his objective. Why get in the way?

Make it easy for him to research, compare, order, ask questions or complain. If you block his natural preferences you will only meet resistance. You will only make things worse. He doesn't want a performance, he wants your service to perform.

The e-customer is not as familiar with your site as you might think. It is rarely the centre of his universe even if you are his ISP or default portal. He views electronic channels as a single resource and will usually be busy moving back and forth between sites and channels to help make his decisions or sate his curiosity.

Use easy-to-understand titles and view your site as just part of a wide web. If you can fit into that view of the world and still ensure that you are relevant then you have a great chance of being seen as useful by the e-customer.

Not only can you do the wrong things, you may also make big mistakes by not doing some really good (as in profitable) things. You must consider how, for the time that you have the e-customer by your side, you are going to:

- Impress him enough that he comes back.

- Keep him with you.

- Make money from him in as many ways as possible.

When you arrive on a site with no worthwhile content, no services and nothing to buy then you know that big opportunities have been missed.

Initial contact with your e-customer

When an e-customer actively seeks out a site he is clearly interested for some reason. It may only be an interest in web design or curiosity, in which case you may only want to show a nice shiny face and let him move on. It's the enthusiast and the possible purchaser you really want. The relationship is with them.

Provide something for them to do. Make sure that they can buy something from you. Ensure that they can search for what they want both on your site and on the web. Facilitate their interaction with your company or with other fellow e-customers. Provide links between this online world and the real one either through links to your own real-world presence or that of someone else.

If you know anything about the e-customer (based on where he has come from or his past activity using your service) then you really should make the best guess you can about his needs. Don't turn it into an assumption by herding the e-customer down a single-lane path. He may act sheepish but if you try to treat him that way he will probably reveal his true wolfish identity.

You should figure out how to help him formulate his own problem – he will appreciate the help. You need to be able to provide as much product information as he needs without overwhelming him. So start with a really informative summary for each product or service using a standard template. Then allow him to dig deeper to suit his need for more information.

Then provide the very best product demonstration you can think of. The e-customer focuses more on text than graphics so this has to include descriptions that evocatively demonstrate the product. But it is still a visual medium. You can show pictures of a product, videos of it in action, customer testimonials on film, or interactive scenarios that show the benefit of even the most intangible service.

It doesn't have to be pushy but the demonstration does have to clarify in the e-customer's mind what the stuff does and why he would want to buy it. And don't be afraid of linking him to other sources of objective information.

This can include the 'Product of the Year' awards website but it might as well also feature the good and bad reviews on a consumer review site (like epinions.com or which.com). The e-customer will not buy if he is unsure. He will remain unsure until he has all the relevant information and a stalled decision is no more profitable than a decision in a competitor's favour.

It's the shopping principle taught by *Miracle on 34th Street*. The film where the department store Father Christmas is asked whether his employer sells wooden trainsets and he replies that they do not but their competitors do. He then gives an easy set of directions to follow so that the little boy and his parents can go and buy it. At first his employers are appalled but it turns out that this approach actually builds trust with the customers that naturally leads to increased sales.

Make purchase and delivery simple for your e-customer

The actual purchase has to be as simple as possible. The e-customer hates to repeat himself. It drives him mad. He would often rather abandon time invested in reaching the purchase decision than type in his details twice. So if he has been there before make it easy.

And if he is a first time e-customer then have some faith. There is no need to ask everything about him on the first date. He will call back. He will be interested. Just find out enough to make sure that there is a second chance to cha-cha.

When a physical item is ordered, then delivery and purchase requires an address and credit card details. It does not require his life history. Let him know that these details will be stored securely so that he does not need to type them in again.

Make it clear when he can expect to see his purchase completed or delivered. He wants to be informed. You want him to feel involved. Let him track the progress of the purchase. Make that information available via as many channels as possible.

Avoid the insensitive mistake of trying to sell more to the e-customer *before* you know that he is happy with his current purchase. It is presumptuous and unwelcome. All too often it will reveal that the electronic marketing process is not as sophisticated as it tries to appear. Better to wait until you have built a favourable impression through delivery.

There should be contact but it should focus on letting the e-customer know what is happening, supporting

"The follow-up e-mail is of

immense value"

them through the sale, and checking to see what you could have improved. The follow-up e-mail is of immense value. Even more so because it is often so poorly utilized. It needs to ask questions and then intelligently and rapidly respond to the answers.

Too often the follow-up e-mail simply builds up an expectation of a level of service that is immediately and irretrievably destroyed when the e-customer attempts to reply. He has taken the time to reply and his effort is shamefully wasted by the service provider failing either to read it or reply to it.

A multi-channel solution?

Let me tell you a true story. It illustrates the importance of a multi-channel solution that has been designed with e-customer needs at its centre.

PART I: Our e-customer wants to buy an all-in-one printer that will allow him to photocopy, scan, fax and print. So he gets in the car and drives to an office equipment showroom, where he has often bought products in the past. Nobody tries to help him but despite this he finds a model that suits him.

He asks a question about a particular technical feature and is told that it is not available. He then tries to buy but is told that the item is not in stock. He asks when it will be in stock and is told curtly that there is no way of finding out and that he will need to 'come back next week' to see if the product has been restocked. He even comments that the system isn't very good but is told, 'that's just the way it is'.

Now in case you are wondering, this is an example of poor service. In fact for an e-customer, like our hero, it is inexcusable service. Waiting until next week is not an option. Our e-customer knows it could be much, much better but he had wanted to buy a product immediately so had risked the real-world store experience.

So let's look at just how badly the retail outlet has messed up. It only had three possible competitive advantages: **press its buttons**, **press his buttons** and **press the flesh.** After this experience, it managed to remove all three. Let me explain.

Press its buttons: First the store can allow the e-customer to try the product before he buys. This is important so that the e-customer can compare products. It is one of the key limitations of electronic channels that they do not easily allow e-customers to feel the goods. The retail outlet must then press home its advantage. It must remind the e-customer on each visit to the store that it can do what the internet cannot do.

Press his buttons: Here the retail outlet can, in principle, allow the e-customer to walk out of the store with the desired product. This is immediate gratification. The internet can only achieve this easily for intangible products like financial services, entertainment, advice or software. Again the store must make its advantages count.

Press the flesh: Finally, the physical store can produce real people to make the experience flexible, human and warm. It can do what computers cannot easily do. It can wink, smile, joke, emphasize and go the second mile.

But the big question is...

But the big question is, 'Can the virtual world pick up the challenge?'. Can it make its advantages count where the real world has failed pathetically and completely? Well judge for yourself in Part II of 'They won't come back next week':

PART II: Our e-customer leaves knowing that the retail outlet could have tried to find out about stock availability. He isn't convinced about the answers he received and wonders why they didn't suggest he use the internet in store or later at home. He is disappointed at the lack of manners shown to him.

He logs on to the internet when he arrives home and deliberately ignores the option of looking up pcworld.co.uk since he hardly wishes them well. Instead he goes straight to the source, the manufacturer's online shopping service. He searches for printers and is shown a model that has all the features that he had been assured were not available while in the shop. It is only marginally more expensive and is available right away.

He then decides to e-mail another supplier of computer products, microwarehouse.co.uk, that has served him well in the past (loyalty effect) to see if it can match the price. He receives an immediate phone call back to confirm availability, a lower price and the fact that it can be delivered the next day by 12 pm. And before he confirms the order his contact on the phone confirms that if he has any problems he can return it immediately. All done and dusted in 30 minutes.

(loyalty effect)

So the virtual world has managed to overcome its 'press the flesh' advantage by linking a real human into the process with full e-customer records so that he could pick up the relationship from where it was left last time. It overcame the 'press his buttons' advantage by delivering it to his office rather than making him haul it around himself. And it overcame the 'press its buttons' advantage by including a returns guarantee. And on top of this it demonstrated additional strengths: lower prices, personalization, information richness, and a full warehouse of products.

In case there is any doubt, the real world was trounced, whipped and beaten into a whimpering, simpering mess. The e-customer is now ten times more likely to stick with the virtual world for future purchases.

Victory

But that was not the end of the war. Virtual businesses have to remember that the first sale is just the beginning – merely an early skirmish. The real world has not disappeared from view and will come back into the frame if the electronic experience lets the e-customer down.

Our story had a number of lows after the initial victory. The printer arrived without the software it needed so that it could not be used. The manufacturer's website promised that the required software would be available in a couple of months time. A couple of months?!

"Simply

Multiple calls direct to the manufacturer were fruitless. Some people didn't have the necessary information. The suggestion from most was to wait for two weeks. Two weeks?! The e-customer didn't pay for this problem. He paid them to give him a printing solution. Every second spent trying to resolve the problem himself diminished the value of that solution.

He eventually turned back to the online intermediary who jumped into the situation and managed to use his influence to obtain the required CD for the next day.

In the end success, but it illustrates the fundamental challenges of using various channels to keep the e-customer buying. It shows that the intermediary is often more motivated by the promise of repeat sales. It also demonstrates the way that the intermediary is still hampered by the product manufacturer.

When two parties work together the overall level of service is often the average of the standards of both parties – perhaps even the lower standard of the two. It takes a concerted effort to ensure that the higher standard prevails.

Provide your e-customer with long-term value and interest

Rarely does an electronic service fail because of purely technological reasons. The technology is just not that unreliable. It's pretty good stuff. It crashes, it embarrasses, it confuses but on the whole it will deliver.

ransferring a **product or a service** to a new channel is **not enough** "

It will fail if the proposition to the e-customer is not considered end-to-end. Success requires thinking the service all the way into the e-customer's life, through the technology, the processes, and the people that facilitate it. Flaws in any of these three areas will weaken the chances of avoiding failure and achieving mega growth.

The idea is not enough. Simply transferring a product or a service to a new channel is not enough. There are plenty of examples where the e-customer experience is positively underwhelming and nothing new is being offered at all. Graphics, media partnerships, PR and advertising will not save the channel if it does not answer the question: 'Why should I bother spending my money and my life using this service?'

Now you may say, our site is open, it's basic, we haven't considered the points that you have mentioned and yet e-customers are still flooding into our site, buying, browsing. Business is booming.

There are a number of explanations: some encouraging and some that are a little more worrying. If they are coming at all it is because you do in fact offer something that they want or at least something that interests them. That is great but it doesn't mean that you are offering anything of long-term value and interest.

It may be that the channel is hot and as a result the need that your site is meeting is simply the curiosity of e-customers. They need to start somewhere and your site is a convenient place. Some e-customers are a long way from being sophisticated users of the medium. They are just starting out (rather like you) and they will turn up because of recommendations from friends or magazines, pure luck, interest in an advertisement or because your brand is recognizable from the real world.

So what happens as they start making comparisons? As they become more confident and knowledgeable. As their basic need to inform and educate themselves is met. They will judge your offering. If it is simple but meets key lifestyle needs better than the competition then 'bravo'. There is no virtue in complication (consider the examples that we have given).

If it does not justify the time that the e-customer has to spend online, the hassle, the waiting, the form filling, then he will simply choose to spend his time (and life) on something else. He may even choose to spend it with you (a brand perhaps he trusts) but using another real-world channel. This is dangerous stuff because suddenly the investment case that you have made for the internet (cost savings in dealing with e-customers) is compromized.

Give a little whistle ...

There are very few tech havens (places that are actually unconnected to the communications world) left. And even they will diminish as the benefits of internet based services increase and the coverage of satellite-based communications widens.

Any global player should seek to be the traveller's friend. They should seek to be the indispensable human extension. Never mind 'have you lost your tongue?', the phrase of the future may be 'have you lost your communicator?'.

To get into the right pocket, into the right ear, into the Jiminy Cricket position in the e-customer's life – this is valuable. And the most likely way into that position is via the mobile phone. Or at least into the evolution of the mobile phone.

Revenues in the mobile communications market are worth billions. But the margins will not stay if the privilege of that Jiminy position is not earned. And that means you had better provide me with content, services, entertainment and, quite literally, wisdom.

This 'wise friend' can already tell you boring things like the weather forecast and interesting things like the result of a championship match. You can order any book you like or be shown a map to the nearest parking space.

Next year it will advance further. Before 2010 is out we will have the integrated provider of all knowledge[50] – the pocket guru. He won't complain about the fluff in your pocket. He will inform, enlighten, and interact in real time to support you.

The e-customer wants to be a superman. To be able to swim in the Mediterranean while beaming back pictures of the multicoloured fish via his rugged, waterproof, personal communicator with built-in web cam and mobile phone modem. Now there is a service worth paying for.

The technologies are available right now to you and to your company. If you used them well you would be ahead of the game. But by only a whisker. But perhaps you will choose to ignore. To procrastinate. To be brutally commercial. There simply are not enough people out there who are using these services. So you conclude that it is not worth your effort.

So answer me this. How can they use them without content? The services need to be there behind the technologies. Someone will get this right. The alternative to being out front is being behind. At some point the gates are locked behind the leaders. The laggards are closed out of the race.

Mobile commerce

The promises for the internet in your pocket are, if anything, more extreme than those for the internet on your desk. For example:

- Your business can be in your e-customer's pocket at all times.[51]

- You can contact your e-customer 24 hours a day, anywhere!

- The mobile is the last element in your firm's supply chain.

- This is cheaper, faster, and can lead to a much closer relationship.

On top of these overwhelming benefits to the business (note that there is little mention of the e-customer in all this), the pundits are keen to point out that the mobile market is, or will become, immense no matter where you are doing business.

The enthusiasm among most of us for mobile phones appears to be insatiable, without an end in sight. Already there are more than 500 million mobile phones in the world. In the UK, a country of only 60 million people, there are more than 27.2 million mobile phone users. That's more than one phone per household!

"The enthusiasm
among most of us

This is all very attractive but you are entitled to ask whether it all adds up. It is not at all certain that the logic that is applied to the m-commerce boom is entirely valid. It is more than possible than the need to achieve sales targets has biased the messages that suppliers of these technologies give to us. More worryingly for your business case, it is probable that your supplier has done little, if any, research into how their technology can make you money. He just knows that, 'you need to get involved now and benefit from first-mover advantage'.

First-mover advantage is very rarely enough to succeed in this or any consumer market. It should also be pointed out that the window of opportunity for simply being first to have a mobile internet service has already passed! So comfort yourself with the thought that it has never been enough to be the first to try. It is far more important to be the first to succeed.

So let's look at the way that the market is going. A mixture of analyzing what *has* happened and *predicting* what will happen.

First, we have already had a wave of mobile explorers (there is even a website dedicated to them at mobilexplorer.com.). These are the pioneers, the trendsetters, those who have either grasped the opportunities presented by the medium or those who have been hoodwinked into investing. They are those who have built the first 50,000 WAP web pages and registered cute domain names with the world 'mobile' or 'wap' included in the title. So we see 'waptastic.com', 'wapscallion.com'.

or mobile phones
appears to be insatiable "

Europe has more mobile phones per person than any place on Earth.[52] It has mobile phones everywhere. They answer a need in the European psyche, lifestyle, and domestic budget. The fight for the mobile e-customer in Europe is fierce and constant. It effortlessly brings hundreds of billions of dollars into the investment pot.

Hmmm … Strange then that the USA has still managed to be ahead in this area in terms of providing the PDA, mobile data communications and usable services that the e-customer might actually want. The most likely explanation is an obvious one, that the US approach is more centred on service and that it is simply transferring service expertise into a new channel.

The European market is busy, loudly and expensively promising 'everything' on billboards, shop windows and television. It is only slowly finding that is worth talking about in terms of new services. Europe remains hooked on cost savings, selling, and growth by acquisition. These are poor ingredients for the creation of killer services – stuff that people would really value and use.

If you really want to make money from mobile technology you either need to be selling it to gullible business people *or* you need to do something worthwhile with it. So let's examine the needs of the mobile e-customer a little more closely and see if we can match his characteristics with those of the technology and create something he will value and pay for.

Create something of value for your mobile e-customer

Mobile e-customers buy their mobile electronic products (little computers and mobile phones) because they feel that they meet some kind of need. This need fits into one of two categories. It could be a **fashion purchase** where the motivation is either to 'look good and up-to-date' or to 'fit in with the crowd'. It could also be a **self-improvement purchase** bought with the belief that it will actually enhance the e-customer's 'ability to do more' or 'ability to do less'.

It is here, right at the heart of the purchase, that you need to build your service or proposition to the mobile e-customer. The mobile e-customer has prioritized the purchase of the mobile device for one or more of these reasons. Services that meet the reasons for purchase will be most likely to be used and bought.

You can write the essential motivators up on the whiteboard (electronic or otherwise), in the form of a mission statement and then as a question:

HOW CAN OUR MOBILE SERVICE BE RECOGNIZED BY OUR E-CUSTOMERS AS MEETING THEIR NEEDS **TO LOOK GOOD, FIT IN WITH THE CROWD,** ACHIEVE MORE AND DO LESS?

The most valued services, and therefore the most successful and profitable, will be those that meet all of these needs simultaneously. You need to get into the head of the target e-customer and figure out what would really turn him on about a service.

The **do less** motivator is crucial in the design of the service, the proposition, and the advertising that goes with it. Any service that saves time, travel, hassle, waiting (or even money) should be considered as a possibility.

It is unfortunately true that an e-customer will be more demanding of your solution because he has to use a machine to achieve it. That's just the way it is. People don't like machines if they make them feel stupid. They also expect more from them because they have seen enough science fiction to know what computers should be able to do.

The satellite-based service from Boeing, Connexion, will allow travellers to access a full range of internet services, e-mail, news and television channels from the comfort of their seat, whilst enjoying the obligatory drink and cruising at 40,000 feet.

" Every year the e-customer

The real benefit comes when the flight crew use the facilities to communicate ahead to amend in-flight service requests to increase e-customer comfort and satisfaction.

Companies such as MapQuest.com are already taking mobile phone use to new heights by building 'device-agnostic' services. The first of these will enable a user to speak into his mobile phone and, for example, request directions or conduct an e-commerce transaction over the phone. The service will respond by delivering personalized information back via any channel of his choice, including on to his mobile phone screen, via fax, e-mail, download, or even answer with its own natural language electronic voice.

Where does your big idea or existing services fit into such a world? Are your systems ready to be integrated into the offering of another company? Can you reorganize your proposition to add value to an e-customer on the move? Every year the e-customer will demand more than he is receiving. Every year a small proportion of companies will move closer to meeting those expectations. Others will simply run out of ideas and expertise.

That's how it always starts

We have to assume that nobody goes out of their way to cause anguish or boredom to those e-customers visiting their electronic presence. And yet that is still what happens to too many unwary life-loving visitors.

If we discount sadism then we are left with two more likely explanations. It is possible that the original pure and enjoyable objectives of the project were hi-jacked by well-meaning, boring,

will demand

more than he is receiving 🙸🙸

visionless committees who translated the thrilling mission of the
e-project into grey, soulless, pedantic slop.

Alternatively the people who set the project up in the first place didn't
have a clue about what e-customers really want and how to translate
that into the electronic medium.

That there should be some misunderstanding or resistance to meeting
the e-customer's needs by a business entity is perfectly natural. This is
because most organizations have fitted 'customer empathy dampeners'
on the doors to their premises.

It appears that they forget that they have ever bought anything as soon
as they enter the building. They switch roles. They are busy looking
after their day job. Accountants look after spreadsheets. Programmers
look after technology. Marketing look after brochures and corporate
events. Many people look after Number One. And Number One is
certainly not the e-customer.

Another reason they forget is that it is simply too painful to try to reach
the e-customer through all the barriers including rules, traditions,
procedures, legalities, incompatibilities, cost and time.

Projects, new initiatives and individual performance should all be
judged on such questions 'whether they add value in the perception of
the e-customer' or 'do they make our e-customer's lives noticeably
better' or 'will the e-customer notice the difference and thank us for it'.

Instead they are judged on whether it cuts costs (this may be good or
bad for the e-customer) or whether it beats the competition (this may
be good or bad for the e-customer).

Many of those responsible for selling to the e-customer are not e-customers themselves. Only a certain percentage of each country's population is actively engaged with electronic channels. This percentage is further reduced in certain age ranges and professions.

This leaves a small minority of people within a business who can be considered experienced e-customers. Even fewer of those are in positions of seniority or influence. This situation should lead to several initiatives within any company serious about competing for e-customer spending.

It is a terrible waste

Start listening to your non-managerial staff – e-customers in your midst

It is a terrible waste to leave your **most qualified e-customers** at the bottom of the pile, excluded from the design and conception of unique service propositions. Just take a look at how many 17–24 year olds are at the base of the organization. They are more likely than anyone to use new electronic devices, channels and services.

Not only the young are neglected but also e-customers of any age. Do you know how e-aware your workforce is? Have you identified the most advanced users of the technologies around which you are trying to reshape your business? Are you sure that they all work in the IT department? What are you doing to plug your company strategy into the experience of the early adopters in your own organization?

Get your credentials as a fully fledged e-customer

If you are going to work out what is possible in this new e-world then there is no better way to do it than becoming part of it. It is just not effective enough to view the new concepts as merely something that can be done at work. There is a reason why so many of the millionaires in the world of dot.com are at the young end of the spectrum and that is because they used the medium sufficiently to be able to apply it to e-customer's needs.

Have you got digital interactive television? Have you used instant messaging? How about 3D chat? Message boards? Video conferencing with a web cam? Shared white boarding? Text messaging via a mobile phone? A WAP based phone? Have you used e-banking? E-retailing? E-medicine? E-careers?

Every company in the world should ensure that someone in the company has access to all these technologies at home. And most should also set up an e-customer suite where the company decision makers can play, order, experiment, become immersed. It is only then that the possibilities start to be understood.

It is ridiculous to attempt to lead an organization forward with no first-hand experience of the tools, concepts, services and devices that deliver the electronic age. In too many companies I find an absence of the basics that an e-customer will come to expect.

Not only is it unimpressive it will simply not work. The benefits of size, mass and sheer numbers of people are being reduced. The key to success lies in being able to meld marketing, technology, operations and people into something efficient and profitable that maximizes the value to the end e-customer.

Implement explicit design and walkthroughs of the e-customer experience

This has always been true, as I keep saying, but it is more true now than ever. Each member of the organization must think through everything from the e-customer's point of view. Does it makes sense to the e-customer? The e-customer has a low tolerance for excuses particularly those that are not communicated to him and those presented electronically rather than by a fellow human being. It is easier to feel empathy and patience with a person than a computer when you know it could be so very much better.

Usability reviews take on new significance. Each and every part of what could be a set of procedures, forms, traditions and attitudes needs to be attacked from the e-customer perspective. Ideal usability is no longer a nice thing to have – it's essential, it's being provided elsewhere, and soon it will be better than ideal. Expectations will be set higher while you are still considering whether to launch 'super average'.

Real people need to use the systems that are being unleashed. Each person in an organization needs to start thinking like a real person, an e-customer, even when they are at work. What is reasonable to demand when you are consuming can seem unreasonable when you are supplying.

It's like the pedestrian versus driver transformation that so many of us have experienced! Have you ever cursed the pedestrian for stepping out in front of you? Have you ever cursed the driver for not simply putting on his brakes earlier?

The golden rule applies to business and more than ever to e-business. Do unto others as you would have done into you. Provide service unto others that you would have given unto you. Sell products unto others as you would have sold unto you. Why more important? There is no excuse for sloppiness when so much has been automated. The company cannot blame cost as the reason when it was rude or thoughtless – it doesn't cost much to automate a thank you!

Don't think that the e-customer will be forgiving because you are just getting to grips with electronic channels. Echoing the beggar in *Fiddler on the Roof* you can see the e-customer shrug and say, 'so you've got growing pains, why should I suffer?'

Survey after survey has shown that the e-customer expects the very best and that he is actively comparing it with the real world. One in five still have more problems online than in-store. One in three have concluded (for now) that it is easier to shop in the mall than on the web.[53]

You will not be surprised to learn that only one third of e-customers are satisfied with their overall shopping experiences.[54] The impact of this is felt immediately at the bottom line as e-customers that are treated poorly become 50% less likely to remain a repeat purchaser. Not satisfying them is an expensive business.

Satisfy your e-customer

There are two vital dimensions required to satisfy the e-customer. The service must have an electronic structure that is **usable** and the process that supports it must have standards of delivery that make it **enjoyable**.

The e-customer will not find your service useful if it is not usable. He interacts with your service through a screen that is littlish (PC), tiny (PDA), or itty bitty (mobile phone). The smaller a space is, the more expertly it must be designed.

That's where the interaction is structured. Sure we're going to work together to get beyond its constraints but it is still a key part of the game. And conceptually the screen will endure even when other communications methods become mainstream.

Typically it starts off as a rectangular space. It is often referred to as real estate when e-customer experience designers are deciding on the fixed purposes of each square inch or centimetre. Tell your designers to keep within the dimensions provided – to avoid excessive scrolling. Make sure you focus on using depth, not width or length.

As the saying goes, 'too many clicks spoil the browse'. It should be possible to find what you want and read, use or buy it with a minimum of effort.

The amazon.com model of selling millions of potential books to a potential e-customer and then trying to sell additional products will become too complicated unless a better way is found of simplifying the choices to an individual.

Search engines are useful, but when faced with so many potential choices the e-customer can become paralyzed. Like an immensely long menu in a new restaurant it is hard even to know where to begin to start. The customer looks for the familiar. He gravitates towards the set menus and the chef's special. Both are familiar concepts that may contain unfamiliar food.

Such devices allow us to use familiar structures to experiment with new things until we find new favourites. These can be ordered by name in the future. The electronic channel equivalent will be needed where choices are so numerous. Consider placing a 'we recommend' banner at the start of your web service to allow people to try something out without searching.

So what is wrong with the idea that electronic services should organize themselves around the e-customer and what the e-customer will be doing? Nothing really but it must be very difficult for some designers to work out. If the system is not usable it will not be used.

A change in viewpoint, perspective, attitude is needed. The technology exists now but is seldom used to its full potential to answer the decades-old ergonomics question: How do we make this easier to use? Despite this expertise, uncomfortable chairs are still produced, cars are still built with the switches in the wrong places, and websites still take too long to load and have no search facilities.

Why? Because they are often designed by engineers not ergonomists. We need a new profession of e-customer experience designer. A combination of marketing, behavioural science, HCI, ergonomics and design skills. One individual able to get into the shoes of the e-customer and design for him.

> **The e-customer understands the difference between class and dross**

We need devices that have been created for people with the e-customer in mind from the start – like the Nokia 8810. Think like Frank Nuovo, Chief Designer at Nokia Mobile Phones. Design something that is technically advanced but that appeals to all the senses:

WE WANTED TO **CREATE A PHONE** WHICH WAS NOT ONLY ABOUT ADVANCED TECHNOLOGY. EVEN **MORE IMPORTANT,** WE WANTED TO DESIGN A PHONE THAT WOULD MAKE PEOPLE INSTINCTIVELY **REACH OUT** AND SAY, **'I LIKE THIS'.** A DESIGN THAT WOULD **COMMUNICATE STYLE** AND ENDURING QUALITY. LIKE A FINE WATCH OR A FOUNTAIN PEN, **THE NOKIA 8810 IS A PRODUCT** YOU NEED. BUT MORE THAN THAT, IT IS A BEAUTIFUL OBJECT **THAT YOU DESIRE.**

Designers would be advised to do far more story-boarding – dreaming up services that create a sense of solidity, and encompass the pleasure of well-designed materials. The e-customer understands the difference between class and dross. He will enjoy the finer points of design even if he can't say exactly what they are.

Don't think that high usability will excuse inattention to **service delivery**. The e-customer wants both. He is already unimpressed with the difference between his (very high) expectations for acknowledgement and response times and the (very low) service standards of many businesses. The e-customer expects an acknowledgement within one hour but only 12% currently have that privilege. Most have to wait 24 hours regardless of how urgent the request. Try an experiment for yourself. Send out ten e-mails with the word 'urgent' and see how long it takes to receive a reply.

Never be taken for granted

Of course excellent service is desirable but to deliver it requires a holistic understanding of what is in the mind of the e-customer. The answers coming back from research into the behaviour of thousands of e-customers make it clear that excellence is a multifaceted concept. It involves many different components.

Aretha Franklin first sang her demand for R.E.S.P.E.C.T in 1967. It became an anthem for political movements including civil rights and feminism. Many e-customers now sing the chorus incessantly, if silently. When online they feel their rights more keenly.

It's no good faking it. **Respect** comes from a profound interest in the e-customer as an individual. As a real person. As an equal. He doesn't come into your store or your interactive TV channel begging you to serve him. That doesn't mean he is always confident. It means that he will not stand being put off, postponed, lied or condescended to.

Another criteria for achieving excellence is **access**. The easier it is to do business with you the more popular you will be. When the e-customer is under pressure he does not like to find that you are 'closed after 5 pm' or uncontactable using the channel that he has available.

So stay open longer, even if it is for emergency only help. This does not need to be expensive if it utilizes outsourced call answering and automated e-mail answering services. The e-customer will not always use the best channel for you but if you make him feel that you are always there for him he will make the extra cost worth your while.

The e-customer also wants **'second mile service'** in such circumstances. He does not want be told that it's against the rules, or that it is too late, or that there is nothing that can be done. He may not be completely unreasonable but dealing with him may feel like it.

Electronic systems tend to be built to follow rules and instructions that are quite rigid. They have seldom been written to cope with exceptions. This means that they usually only go the first mile. They do what is expected and nothing more.

Your challenge is to design processes that allow exceptions to be made in support of the e-customer so that they really get what they want to pay for. It's the best way of ensuring that they continue to pay. This most often means letting those pesky people back into the process to cope with additional demands. But it also means allowing flexibility in the technology platforms that support such requests and in the guidelines that encourage people to go out on a limb for an e-customer.

There will be many moments of truth along the way that give you the opportunity to impress the e-customer. To show that you are on his side. You need to be ready to make the most of them. You can even go further and create such occasions by setting the promise deliberately lower than the ability to deliver.

This means planning what we can call 'four-day weeks' for systems and people – to allow slack in the system and then actively seek ways of using it up in delivering miracles to your e-customers.

Every problem is an opportunity for a business. Many existing .com ideas were inspired by the difficulties that their founders have had with real-world and virtual-world services. Unfortunately the ideas do not solve problems that are valuable enough or the service would have been better delivered.

Imagine how you could sell the service via advertising. Think through whether you can explain succinctly the benefits that your service will bring. If you cannot explain it then it is unlikely to sell itself.

Unless of course you would choose not to explain the benefits of anaesthetic to a patient awaiting surgery. Check with your colleagues. You may have found a fantastic idea and lack the eloquence to explain it.

To serve the e-customer you should not be a technologist or an accountant at heart. Let those guys do what they do. Those people should be serving you while you figure out a way of serving the end e-customer. You need to get the bits together and assemble them into useful stuff that the e-customer will actually want to use.

An affair to remember

As we have already seen, personalization (although still not common) is a necessary component of successful e-customer service, but contact differentiation goes further. It aims to change the deal with each individual e-customer based on his previous requirements. More importantly it means considering how the e-greeting and continued contact can be made more distinct. You want it to be clear each time that they have been dealing with you.

You want the e-customer to enjoy and look forward to your differences and eccentricities. Pop singers seldom perform their songs in a straightforward way. Instead they shout, growl, and pose alluringly. They seek to demonstrate a clear difference between themselves and any other pop pretender. Where an act is a complete replica of an existing band the chances for its long-term survival are diminished. These acts soon fade from view.

Once you have decided how to differentiate your dealings with e-customers – whether wild and wacky, fun and friendly, efficient and effective, jumping and joyous – you will need a culture that reflects the tone, style and substance of the brand.

For an idea of how to match tone to e-customer state of mind, try the film-script site, script-o-rama.com, where Drew is deservedly well known for 'chatty, informal prose that makes him seem like an old buddy'.[55] An extract will illustrate the point:

I KNOW THERE'S A GROUP OF YOU **CRAZED MARMOT.**
PROBABLY GROWING TIRED OF MY TELLING YOU **GO TO** THE OTHER SIT
'I DIDN'T EVEN REALIZE YOU HAD A REDESIGNED SIT
YADDA'. AS IS MY PHILOSOPHY IN ALMOST EVERY WALK IN LIF
YOU HAD A CHOICE IN THE FIRST PLACE

The best companies push brand through the entire organization, certainly the whole service organization. So that processes, complaints handling, products, website, TV channel, tone of voice all fit the advertising.

If the realities of the advertisement only exist in the head of your marketing communications manager then it may fool the e-customer once or twice. But you are missing a great opportunity to build trusting relationships, and handing the initiative over to the competition.

Don't rely on being able to schmuzzle and confuse the e-customer. There are two constructive approaches. You could **open up** to the e-customer. Be as honest and clear as you can be about the meaning of value proposition. Ensure that all terms and conditions are stripped of their legalese and explained as clearly as possible. Ask your legal guys for a rewrite until a child of 12 could understand them all without thinking too hard. Let them know when there is a better option available. No one will thank you for letting them buy in error.

Alternatively you will have to find a way of **reducing the workload** for the e-customer so that all he has to do is hand over the money, having been entertainingly and effortlessly sold your stuff.

Use of easy 'how-to guides' can help by letting the e-customer sit back and enjoy the show. These can be constructed like self-running slide shows using web pages, or video (QuickTime), or animation

HAT **ACTUALLY CHOOSE** TO COME TO THIS SITE, AND YOU'RE

BUT HEY, I KEEP HAVING PEOPLE E-MAILING ME SAYING

ECAUSE I HAD A SPECIFIC PAGE BOOKMARKED, **YADDA YADDA**

M COOL WITH EITHER CHOICE YOU MAKE, AS LONG AS YOU KNOW

HAVE A FEELING THE **TENSING ON THAT SENTENCE**

IS REALLY WRONG...

(macromedia.com). They can guide an e-customer down easy-to-use decision trees or even along 'as simple as you can make them' non-decision poles.

The involvement of real live people can move the web away from being a self-service channel into being a service-led channel. It won't suit everyone but it has the advantage of helping the e-customer over objections and concerns. Often lack of information or lack of confidence prevents the e-customer from buying.

Forcing the e-customer to duplicate effort is morally wrong and commercially damaging. It slows down the sale and allows doubt to spring up in the mind of the 'otherwise happy to buy' e-customer. He should be reminded just before the confirmation of sale that there is no need to re-enter details. It's a great time to emphasize the simplicity and security that this provides him with as a 'valued e-customer'.

In reality, the two approaches can be even more effective if they are complementary. Making the whole experience as hassle-free as possible. Smoothing away all friction between the first sign of interest and the sale, while at the same time being open, clear, honest and friendly.

You need to understand what the e-customer feels subconsciously. He is put on edge by legal jargon. He is made skittish if all the information is not available. But he does not wish to read through it all before he can buy.

Avoiding icky sticky
It is important to make sure that the e-customer spends as long as possible at your site without him ever deciding that his time has been wasted. This means that the process must be efficient but strewn along its path must be as many distractions as possible.

You should be quite happy if he hangs around to browse and chat. Each second you keep him interested and happy is another second to convince him to buy and to return. Something must grab his attention and encourage him to stay.

The preference is to leave the choice to him to stay or go but make the diversions so attractive (and possibly useful in their own right) that he feels happy with his choice. There are so many ways of catching his eye that you do not even have to overreach the bounds of decency to achieve your goal.

Catching your e-customer's eye

For starters, you have **games and puzzles**. Some, like the fun 'ping pong' arcade, available at the UK bank virtual bank cahoot.com, are playable online or downloadable. Simple, fun and branded they provide a perfect and inexpensive way of holding the e-customer's attention for long periods. They also link the brand with added value for very little extra investment.

Competitions can be run on their own as a simple 'register to have a chance of winning' competition like the BT 'win a million' (costing only about 5 cents or 3 pence per e-customer). They can also run as competitions for winners of quizzes or games. This can be as simple as the 'best score' every day, week or month, or as sophisticated as a fantasy league that rewards people whose teams succeed.

Either way such competitions have in common the ability to gather registration details. You can't win without typing in your contact details. They encourage repeated visits to the site to determine the current position of the competition.

They also open up a simple and acceptable way of starting up an outbound relationship with the e-customer. A registration e-mail is the first to be sent. This reassures the e-customer that the company can deal efficiently with electronic support. There follow e-mails to tell him about the latest highest scores and bit by bit he is fed extra snippets of information to be read while he is in learning mode.

The **newsletter** can also be offered on its own terms as a desirable source of news. A number of tough choices are involved that are often best determined with experience. How often should it be sent? Who is going to produce it? What should it contain?

There are many schemes out there that can collate e-mail addresses ready for you to use. There are also many software solutions that provide the same facilities in-house. The challenge is in determining the contents and the production responsibilities.

If the stuff you sell is essentially boring then you may want to consider building a newsletter from stories relating to other areas of interest. A general purpose newsletter that can be customized to the e-customer's views complete with your branding – a pretty useful combination.[56]

Ideal for keeping the e-customer's mind on your brand is **'ticker tape'** software. This feeds the e-customer live news in real time just like old-fashioned ticker tapes. Examples of them in the real world include the ticker that comes with aol.com instant messenger or the one that is provided by bbc.co.uk. Both keep the e-customer thinking about the relevant brands. They also link the sophistication and breadth of the world's news with your products and services.

Demonstrations of selected products allow you to tell the e-customer about the interesting aspects of your product or service. He came to your site or channel deliberately. This means that, in principle, he would like to buy something that he thought you might sell. In this circumstance it seems a pity not to promote the best that the company has to offer.

It's a great way of weaving multimedia into the sales process. Suddenly it does not seem like an imposition, it is part of the benefit of using the site. For extra spice your demonstration can be 3D or it can involve a personality to do the demonstrating. Once the e-customer has made the decision to watch he will be willing to wait for the download times required for film quality demonstrations. He will do this without complaining and with something akin to baited breath.

Similarly, **information** about your products or industry can be very interesting to your visiting e-customer. It helps if you lay it out neatly and attractively. Organizing it via nifty headlines that encourage exploration is sensible.

Further interactivity

Any enhancement to interactivity is to be applauded. Providing **voice chat** for instance will increase the duration of an e-customer's visit to your site from under 30 seconds to an average stay of 40 minutes.

Voice chat has also been shown to increase the conversion of browsing to buying. It helps to tackle the 65% of e-customers who give up the ordering process just before purchasing. Speaking to someone at that point is crucial in getting their business – you need someone empathetic and knowledgeable to discuss it all through with the e-customer.

If you know who they are via the initial details, you can even provide a closer match to the e-customer's age, gender and education profile. It's a superb trick to suddenly be speaking to someone your own age and gender who is knowledgeable and prepared to answer all your questions.

Web cams offer a cute way of opening up your world to theirs. A useful further means of building some kind of happy relationship between e-customer and business. They can show what is happening in the office, factory, shop or club. Everyone loves to peak and a web cam gives them that ability.

Equally, the web cam can be used to provide two-way visual communication. It's a cool feature to offer. It costs very little. It allows the e-customer to play with his own toys without having to hang out in public web chat rooms that are so often unpoliced and open to the advances of the dodgy and depraved.

Providing online **product tracking** is a hot sticky feature because it reinforces so many other messages. It's fun to watch the progress of your order as it works its way through the system. It's impressive to track it as it travels across countries all the way to the e-customer's door.

At the same time it underlines the control and value of the service and provides a fantastic opportunity for the e-customer to show off such a great feature via his phone, TV or PC. It also reduces the number of calls made 'just to check that it is on its way'.

Customers like to customize

It appears that one of the strongest urges of 21st-century man is to **customize**. He can't get enough of individuality no matter how vile, trivial or tacky. Screen savers. Wallpaper. Wacky mobile phone covers. Sites dedicated to downloadable images and ringing tones to reflect your personality just a little more closely.[57]

It's an up and coming trend in the e-customer's world. Providing the ability to change the colours, styles of images, the news that is shown, the greeting that is shown as you enter the site or a thousand other features. It's hot stuff. It keeps the e-customer playing around with your site. He is taking up the challenge to 'make himself feel at home'. And when your site becomes more like home the e-customer is likely to stick around.

The e-customer can already choose to redecorate his software with what are known as **skins**. New web browsers and many of the cooler software applications will have the ability to customize the look and feel of many features.[58]

You can provide your own skins either featuring your own logo or corporate colours for the e-customer to customize his browser, and make them available on your site. Or you can provide skins that allow your own site to be customized. A bank, for example, that is coloured to look like the e-customer's favourite sports team – Citibank in Chicago Bulls colours and images. This kind of stuff wows whole sections of the e-customer world. And the cynics secretly play with it as well.

Creating an experience that allows the e-customer to do what he needs
to while inviting him to stay and play a while. That's the essence of the
approach. Electronic channels provide endless diversions that could
not be provided easily in the real world. Cool links, fun stuff to try out,
bizarre facts, calculators, product reviews, news, animations, free stuff,
stuff to send to your friends, bargains and innovations.

Can't you do it the way I like it?

Come on! Give the
e-customer what he wants and stop messing him about. There is
nothing very enjoyable about spending money on stuff that isn't quite
right because he can't buy it the way he wants it.

> " **Come on!** Give the e-customer
> what he wants and **stop messing
> him about** "

Personalization

Personalization should mean exactly that. It must take the scope of
'personal' marketing beyond a glorified mailshot that proves only that
you can merge the e-customer's name with your form letter or web
page. It is of very little use knowing what he wants if you cannot
deliver it.

Attempts to personalize come across as crass and unsophisticated if the
service or product remains unchanged. Organize the business so that
the e-customer can choose from a combination of all available features
to create exactly what he wants to buy. Design the electronic service so
that the level of choice being offered is immediately apparent and

accessible. Make him understand that the pleasure and privilege of the purchase was all his.

The Barbiettes of the world can create unique dolly divas on barbie.com. Pink flowers and sparkling white stars provide a virtual world to match her real-world 'personality'. Following seven easy steps, it is possible for the mini e-customer to choose from a range of 76,000 combinations including faces, eyes, lips and hairstyle. Next step – save your unique creation and get mum or dad to make that order.

Elsewhere, customestore.co.uk allows the older e-customer of more refined taste to order up a tailor-made shirt to his exact requirements, style, and measurements. You can even have a personalized car made in under three days as a result of pioneering work done in the UK.

If dolls, shirts and cars can be made to order, why not your stuff or services?

If the e-customer can't have what he wants made to measure then he can at least get someone else to shop around for him. Meet the Bots – Advice, Hot, Compare and Finder – cute digital versions of the Tele-tubbies or the Clanger's sophisticated cousins. They have been put into the virtual world to help the e-customer. They exist only to serve.

They are the personalization of technology's ability to search, compare and filter information. If you want to find the best price for a product anywhere on the web then you can simply ask the relevant Bot to do the biz. To find the cream of the cracking deals out there in 'ether, ether land'.

Simply type in what you want and click. Moments later the little compère Bot, dressed up to impress in shiny yellow, will deliver the list of stuff that matches your request.

Science fiction nonsense? No, just visit valuemad.com. Launched in partnership with ASDA (Wal-Mart's latest acquisition in the UK) it promises:

A NEW, **SAFE WAY TO SHOP** ON THE INTERNET …

WHATEVER YOU WANT TO BUY – FROM TVS TO CDS, FLOWERS TO FRIDGES – VALUEMAD

TRACKS DOWN THE BEST DEALS FOR YOU,

BY **COMPARING PRICES** ACROSS AN EVER-WIDENING

RANGE OF WEBSITES … CREATES A RESULTS TABLE OF **THE BEST DEALS,**

SO **YOU CAN DECIDE** WHAT YOU WANT TO BUY, FROM WHOM AND

AT WHAT PRICE!

IT WILL ALSO DIRECT YOU TO ITS **APPROVED** PARTNERS – SITES

THAT HAVE BEEN **VETTED BY US** FOR SECURITY AND **EXCELLENT**

CUSTOMER SERVICE. SO THAT, AS WELL AS **SAVING YOU MONEY.**

VALUEMAD PROVIDES

PEACE OF MIND.

Useful. But is it a shopping experience? That depends on how the Bot
shares its results. It could just be a one-liner … or a link. Better still if it
is a full, rich experience along the lines of 'you'll never guess what I
found' accompanied by a demonstration of the product. Put together it
could sound something like this:

>> " **Max,** I have something for you … on
your mobile phone. "

>> "What is it? "

>> "You know that second honeymoon cruise to **Hawaii for less**

than $1000. **I found it.** Leaving the day before your anniversary. **I can book it now** and have tickets in a beautiful card delivered by Thursday. **Shall I go ahead?"**

 "**Sure.** Can I have travel insurance arranged as well?"

 "**No problem.** I can find **a great deal** to last the rest of the year for not much more than the cost for a week."

 "Does that fit into our spending and savings plans?"

 "**Of course.** I have checked over the figures and it will end up saving you $100 dollars a year. **Shall I go ahead?"**

"**Please do.** And could you make sure that card for the honeymoon has my signature in it with an appropriate verse from her favourite poet?"

"**Already taken care of.** Take care and **have a great day."**

Is any part of this impossible? No. Any of it improbable? No. Does such a service exist? No. Does the service industry lack imagination? Very probably.

Fantastic elastic

Service organizations will grow up that will enable demand for ordering and delivery to be met continually. Production will be the only variable. Let me explain. There is a

"Avoid
being caught up in the
world wide wait"

Natural Wheat & Barley Cereal

relatively finite amount of purchasing power in the world at any one time. There is also a finite amount of time to view and order products. This means that if there was only one shop to order from it would be relatively easy to build a process and an infrastructure that could cope with the total demand for dealing with orders, complaints, payments, deliveries and returns.

This is how postal delivery services work. They know how many homes there are and organize delivery men to deliver each day to a certain percentage based on the general level of demand. Most of the time there is sufficient slack built into the system to cope with demand blips. This may just mean the delivery people working a little faster or longer occasionally.

If people want to get stuff to your house, the good news is that there are only so many homes out there. If people want to answer your questions, the good news is that there is a limit to how many you can ask at any one time. This means that service organizations should grow up that can cope with all of the demand.

The only variation comes from which front-end organization is pushing the demand through the fulfilment system. As a result you should have happy e-customers – whatever they want they get. The trick is to worry about attracting the demand your way.

Buy.com have followed this 'pure model' in pursuit of the e-customer because it believes that in time it will allow them to win. It has chosen to integrate its own systems and processes into those of its six world-class distribution partners. The result is that it has a remarkable ability to increase the scale of its sales without having to follow a traditional cycle of making a business case, investing and then building.

Delivery mechanisms need to be fast enough

The average person spends more than two years of his life in line, waiting and queuing. People jostling in the airport. Pushing into line and along lines for tickets and checking-in. Lines for boarding the plane. Lines for collecting luggage. Lines for taxis. More lines than Hollywood.

On the internet there is no need for jostling. From the e-customer's point of view it doesn't matter whether he is the first or the 6 billionth person wanting to be served. He can be accommodated. Your problem in serving him comes when the 'no jostle promise' cannot be met by a 'no jostle delivery'.

E-customers will be unnecessarily disappointed when their queue of one is impacted by hundreds of thousands of other individuals. Broadband may cure the problem from the e-customer's side of the equation but carefully thought through expandable systems need to be put in place on the business side. Delivery mechanisms on the business side need to be fast enough.

Running up to its launch, Cahoot, the new UK financial services e-service, used a combination of viral e-mail campaigns, leaflet distribution, competitions, and a teaser website. All designed to push e-customers on site to pre-register and then open accounts with them. During the launch they even threw in an unnecessary poster campaign to promote the 0% APR credit card.

Result? Well surprisingly enough it was popular. Credit for nothing has always had its advocates. But after all that preparation and all that advertising, led by the slogan 'Defy Convention', the systems were not able to cope with the demand.

E-customers received error messages (not good for the nervous e-customer or for the demanding e-customer) and could not register. The system did not cope gracefully and did not explain what to do. No reassurance.

The next day e-mails were sent out to pre-registered Cahoot e-customers. The text explained that:

MANY APOLOGIES FOR ANY INCONVENIENCE THAT THE DELAY IN APPLYING **MAY HAVE CAUSED YOU.** **P.S.** IF YOU HAVE **RECENTLY COMPLETED** YOUR APPLICATION, PLEASE IGNORE THIS E-MAIL AND ACCEPT OUR APOLOGIES **FOR TROUBLING YOU.**

Not a good start. Just count the mistakes. The system could not distinguish between those e-customers who had had problems and those who had not. Its 'one message for all' approach meant that e-customers who were not aware of the problem were made fully aware of it. The e-mail communicated the mistake and made it bigger!

So take note. Avoid being caught up in what is being called the world wide wait. The e-customer might as well queue in the real world. It's easier on the eyes.

How do you smile over the web? The human touch is
going to come back into fashion. It will (yet again) become the differen-
tiating factor between services. Computers can deliver lousy service
pretty much on their own. The very best of humankind needs to be
coaxed and coached out into the open. People need to be showcased
and supported.

On the way to the virtual world some businesses have a lapse of
memory – it's a kind of 'Honey, I forgot the people' approach. Others
adopt an *Animal Farm* like 'machine is good, people are bad'
approach. If they adopt the attitude of pigs they should expect to end
up as bacon.

Every business should understand that at heart the internet is not a
machine, it's the interaction of millions of people.[59] In the end
someone still says 'I have something for you to buy' and someone still
replies 'I would like to buy it'. The technology simply represents one
set of people trying to sell to another group of people.

There is the person who runs the business – responsible for its culture,
objectives and stance on service. Then there are the people who design
the processes and the electronic services that the e-customer must use to
deal with them. Don't forget the people who actually make the stuff that
the e-customer wants to buy. Or the people that the e-customer meets
who actually do stuff for him. They all matter and they are all involved.

Unless business is very careful it will put layers of technology in
between buyer and seller in such a way that the connection between

" Every business **should understanc**

them is broken. Ask yourself a few questions: How do you smile at an e-customer over the internet? How do you exchange friendly chat and human warmth through a TV screen? How do you sense that an e-customer is confused, needs help or is unhappy through a WAP phone?

The culture, processes, training and recruitment all need to deliver the appropriate human capacity or characteristic that the e-customer will appreciate. He wants better and better personal service the less human contact he receives.

The advertising has made promise after promise. These people need to deliver their part of the promises that have been made. Sometimes the e-customer deals with flawless e-systems and then 'Wham!' He runs into the brick wall of poor human servants.

Play your human card

Often the involvement of real live people is left too late in the e-customer experience because they are seen as a last resort by a business that thinks the best way of making money is to remove the human touch. The best, most human e-customer experiences should use technology to make people even greater servants.

Business must determine where to place people in order to gain the greatest benefit for all involved. Try a new (dangerous) thought, 'maybe the best time to get people together is whenever they want to talk'.

that at heart the internet
is not a machine,
it's the interaction of millions of people "

Some businesses are beginning to think like this after using 'click to talk' features like humanclick.com. Listen to one rave review:

YOUR SERVICE IS ONE OF THE **GREATEST INVENTIONS OF ALL TIME!** **I'M ABLE TO KEEP PEOPLE** ON MY SITE FOR TEN TIMES AS LONG AS BEFORE, BY **INVOLVING THEM IN CHAT.** I'M SURE SALES WILL **SKYROCKET** AS WELL.

Throw out that anti-human prejudice! The virtual world is not about removing the people. Build in real relationships, feedback loops and achieve continuous improvements to the proposition and its delivery by really getting people involved.

Make sure that the service is able to move smoothly from human to system to human again. If your systems let your people down then your people will be put under pressure. If they do not feel motivated and fulfilled then they will respond to such pressure by siding with the e-customer against the system and, by extension, against the business.

Once you start to rely on the best of human abilities it will be necessary to create incentives, culture, roles and management that gain your people's goodwill. It will require your people actually to care about the objectives of the company and about the needs of e-customers. People rarely empathize with others if they are worrying about their own lack of fulfilment.

What happens to turn decent people into those that serve me badly? They must start the day as reasonable human beings but something happens as they put on the uniform. Something cultural. Something less than desirable.

Experience has shown that more than half of your e-customer services team are unhappy. It is not a revered profession and its standing is likely to diminish further at just the time when the demands of the job are increasing. Unhappy workers will invariably and eventually lead to unhappy customers. A lesson learned and forgotten a million times first by old economy firms and now by many anti-people, new economy start-ups. It is a lesson succinctly explained by Rosetta Riley, Director of Customer Satisfaction, at General Motors:

ONE OF THE THINGS WE LEARNED ... IS THAT THERE'S A **STRONG CORRELATION** BETWEEN EMPLOYEE SATISFACTION AND CUSTOMER SATISFACTION. IF YOUR **EMPLOYEES ARE UNHAPPY** AND WORRIED ABOUT THE VARIOUS BASELINE, **BASIC NEEDS,** YOU KNOW, OF THE QUALITY OF THEIR WORK LIFE,

THEY WON'T WORRY ABOUT CUSTOMERS.

This is why meeting the e-customer's expectations demands an e-culture. That doesn't necessarily mean that free, open, democratic and empowered organizations have to deliver via an electronic front. It does mean that if you deal via an electronic front you're going to need a human at your back who cares what happens. Without them you will not be able to compete.

At what point should the important (and expensive) human card be played? Call centres, live text chat, letters written by people, and even the personal home visit can all play a significant part. Plugging people into the e-customer experience is the vital point at which virtual and real worlds meet.

As technology becomes more and more powerful it may be that people continue to provide its most acceptable face. The e-customer may still not want to deal with all the technology himself. He will desire its benefits but not want to involve himself directly with all of it. Technology can 'magnify the man' but the e-customer may prefer to be magnified indirectly via his human agents.

"

The e-customer may still

Demand high standards from your service representatives

Make people smarter! The abilities of real people delivering service to the e-customer services person will need to increase so they can add value to what the system already provides. If service representatives are left innumerate and illiterate, unable to organize, disaffected and reluctant, they will probably not add anything positive to the service experience. The bar is raised for those able to justify their involvement in the process. It has already started to happen.

Is there a future where we will go to one man to buy everything? A man who is wired into the complete network and is fantastically adept at manipulating the available tools to get us what we need. He may be able to serve and support thousands of e-customers because each needs personal involvement so seldom.

The e-customer is prepared to put up with the (possibly very good) system but when it cannot do what he needs he expects superb human assistance. The e-customer will believe more in the system when exceptions are dealt with swiftly, competently and wisely. He will assume that the rest of the time it is working without human intervention.

The more distant the human representatives are the more important contact with them is. You may only ever see the e-customer representative on three occasions: in time of crisis, time of triumph or when there are public relations possibilities. Rather like a politician.

ot want to deal
with all the technology himself "

You think that I am exaggerating? Perhaps, but we can still examine the immediate need for your people to deal with multiple channels. Several great debates are ongoing as a result between the relative merits of self-service and human services. The call centre and the web. Having people supporting the relationship who expertly deal only with one channel. Or training agents to deal with all channels. The debate will continue.

You need to consider what your existing agents can cope with. Once you consider the cost of involving a human in the process you will want to ensure that they add the highest possible value. If a person, after training, cannot cope with more than one channel it is questionable whether they will be able to add the desired significant value to the system.

They will need high skill levels – more than just talking and managing ten words per minute on the keyboard. They need to know how to navigate on the internet, type at a reasonable speed without significant spelling mistakes and deal with voice calls to meet very specific objectives.

Cool technology does not make people efficient or pleasant. Just watch an inefficient check-out clerk using a sophisticated cash till. It will take longer for you to buy your goods than it would take an efficient clerk to use a simple manual till.

Remember your e-service will still be delivered by people somewhere down the line. If you go outside your own country you will be more reliant than ever on people. Time to think about common training, processes and standards.

Full-time humans can be supplemented by digital personalities or avatars but not replaced. Such services can provide the e-customer with the details and the offers and the headlines that he wants in a way that is easy to digest. Personalization without being bombarded with unwanted choices – that's the ideal.

The first commercial applications have already started, such as the computer-generated newsreader on ananova.com, that can deliver information 24 hours a day with a full range of human characteristics based on Victoria Beckham, Kylie Minogue and Carol Vorderman.

Such advances will continue to be made as the technology becomes faster. We will be able to digitize ourselves to read the news which will make us sound very clever. We may be faced with pop-star images trying to sell us life insurance.

Building trust and integrity

As more choice is delivered to the e-customer he becomes fussier. This can translate into complaints but it can also translate into being more choosy about the kind of people he deals with. Where the morals and ethics of all available suppliers are interchangeable this won't matter very much. But some companies are already noticing the advantages of having integrity and building the business around it.

Listen to Anita Roddick from bodyshop.com:

NOT ONLY MEETING **LEGAL OBLIGATIONS** BUT ALSO THOSE OF **HONOUR.** THE BUSINESS HAS TO **INVOLVE THE COMMUNITY.** **IT SHOULD AVOID** THIS MYOPIC PURSUIT OF COMPETITIVENESS AND TREAT ALL **EQUALLY** THAT HAVE A **STAKE IN THE SUCCESS** OF THE BUSINESS.

The net and the web were both born with altruistic ideals. It is a very wise e-customer flower that includes in his array of fragrances and colours the very attractive 'We have standards. We want to help the world' approach.

E-customers are basically on your side. They want it to work. There may be a few grumpy ones out there, but on the whole they want the stuff that they buy to do the job it was bought for. There must be some failure fetishists around but they do not represent the majority.

But the e-customer does want to deal with people he can trust. People that he likes. So unshrink the people and let them connect – so that you can profit.

Hearing gibberish
When you redesign business for any reason it demands an understanding of multiple disciplines. The more radical the change, the more essential it is to have a comprehensive and deep cohesion between each element of the organization.

There is no time to be a Luddite. Technology is no longer an option, it is inherently wrapped up with the proposition and the service delivery. If you don't understand it, if you have to wait for a game of technology vs business requirements ping-pong, then you continually run behind the best of the competition.

It is not unusual for good ideas to be delayed for months while business and IT try to understand each other. Each to some extent hiding behind their expertise (of their own area) and their ignorance (of the other person's area).

There are some innovations that can only be created if *all* elements of the business mix are inside the same head of at least one person in the meeting. Because people do not tend to innovate in areas they do not understand. They often find it difficult to cope with the basic change needed in the system, let alone move ahead of the current level of thinking.

If your people do not know the way, then they cannot lead the e-customer through electronic channels. The guide must know the way. It doesn't matter one jot whether you or your colleagues find this stuff interesting or not. Just think about your e-customers and not yourself! They need many guides to get the most out of a networked world that is surrounding them.

66 The guide **must** know the way 99

In a world where some people forget to take out hands-free sets from their phones and continue to talk, you are going to need a crash course to get your team up to date. Leaders must know where they are going so it is not enough for them to have used some of it. It is not acceptable for them to decide that they don't personally like it.

Not everyone will be able to recruit people who inherently understand all the technology. And even if you could they would not necessarily understand the business in enough detail. What you need are people with a full grasp of the constraints but a belief that they are there to be overcome.

There are a lot of people who are doing a lot of talking without really understanding the issues. A lot of people pretend to know what they are talking about.

There are scared, obfuscating employees and managers and consultants who have learned the appropriate e-speak and potentially the technology but have failed to grasp the essentials. They have come to it late and try to make up for it by setting their mouths to 'internet speed' (make a mental note not to trust those who use the term). They think the internet was created in 1997 and only ever quote amazon.com as an example.

There are others who reject vital information that sounds like gibberish to them because they do not understand it. Sure, it's pretty alien to the average business person. But when the extraterrestrials have landed its time to think alien thoughts. And a great time to learn alien languages.

Consider the experience of Times Warner, a $110-billion old media company, that realized it had to get involved in the new media future. Early attempts included a $100-million interactive television project that simply did not work, the failure to invest in yahoo.com and aol.com when they were fledgling companies and the disastrous 1994 launch of pathfinder (described as 'a poster child for old media cluelessness').[60]

In 1997, an entertainment site, entertaindom.com that sought to be the centrepiece of web strategy linked to other hubs around it, was put forward. The success of yahoo.com led Times Warner to put one of its best people in charge, a man who had been described as a 'genius' at making money.

Unfortunately, Richard Bressler was now playing the money-making game in a language that he did not understand. The joke was that he would be deciding the digital strategy on the same day his secretary taught him to use e-mail. He did not understand firewalls, server farms, bandwidth constraints or hubs. He did not grasp the essential nature of this brave new world.

Result? They launched more than a year late. They lost key people. Their competitors had moved in. They had to merge with AOL. The smaller company will now take control. This failure occurred in large part because an intelligent man and the board above him did not speak gibberish fluently.

Times Warner are not alone. When speaking to groups of senior executives, I invariably ask questions about their personal knowledge of the services and technologies that surround the e-customer. Their answers reveal that only 20% have used an internet chat room, only 30% have used a web cam, only 16% have used a mobile internet phone, only 15% have used a an mp3 player, and a mere 25% have tried out shopping via interactive television.

Are you alarmed by those figures? If the leaders haven't been there then how can they lead anyone else? If you don't know what the technology can do then how can you move ahead of the competition? It is not possible to inspire the e-customer or the technology workers without a deep understanding of the components and the culture.

Make the technology work for your e-customer

The technology can do anything that you want it to do. If your technology advisors say anything else then you are being poorly advised. And there is a lot of poor advice out there given by those who are out of date. Maybe those who were never really up   to date.

They simply don't get it. The difference between the superb and the average is immense. Just because the guy in front of you can say and understand words that you struggle with does not make him the person to trust. It's worth paying huge premiums to get the best.

This book is more interested in what the technology can do than the details of the technology itself. But just for completeness we thought we would include a 65-word shopping list that should be enough for you to ask for the technology that your e-customers need:

AN E-BUSINESS PLATFORM THAT WILL **SUPPORT THE PROCESS** AND PEOPLE **THAT DELIVER** THE E-BUSINESS PROPOSITION. CAPABLE OF BEING **CHANGED RAPIDLY** AND ALLOWING E-CUSTOMERS TO **CREATE PERSONALIZED** PRODUCTS AND SERVICES. ONE THAT INTEGRATES **CUSTOMER COMMUNICATION** AND RELATIONSHIP MANAGEMENT OVER MULTIPLE CHANNELS **INCLUDING** THE INTERNET, INTERACTIVE TELEVISION, VOICE, BRANCH AND MOBILE WIRELESS **DEVICES.** ONE THAT IS **CAPABLE OF INTEGRATING** CUSTOMER-FACING SYSTEMS WITH SUPPORT SYSTEMS AND **BACK-END SYSTEMS.**

Without such a system even some of the mighty electronic only brands may find themselves as poorly placed to exploit real-world locations as the powerful real-world brands have been to exploit new electronic channels. The new winners will be those who have recognized the importance of serving the e-customer across multiple channels in a myriad of ways. Multi-channel companies that build technology systems and attitudes that can cope with innovations, that actively seek change and improvement.

You need the best people

If a business does not understand the new technology or its differences then it will need the help of those who do. Unfortunately the best brains, the best implementers, the quirkiest, the zaniest, the most valuable innovators no longer want to work for businesses that do not get it.

Business will have to learn to love them, challenge them, and reward them. Fun, life, work, respect are all on their must-have lists. They know that there is a better way and are not prepared to play 15 years of company politics to put it into action.

While the bitter cynics wait for the failed optimists to return to the fold from their dot.com adventures, something has already changed forever (or as long as we will both live which is long enough). Everyone with the talent or the belief has seen a better more exciting way.[61] And that will not simply disappear because of a heavy slump in new economy stocks.

If you treat these people as they were before they left, you will lose their real attention permanently. Even if you get them back, the creative drain away from innovation for your company to other projects may well continue.

It's a problem that besets business and even nations. France has lost 30,000 of its top IT people to the US over the past five years. Every year it loses 20% of its graduates from the Grandes Écoles. It is not only that there is more money in Silicon Valley, it is that there is more belief in possibilities and dreams.

The fight for the e-customer demands the best, motivated people at every level of the business. It is a fight for talent. The grooming of talent. Attract and retain the team so that they can attract and retain the e-customer.

They want as much as the e-customer, maybe more. They want to belong to something with a heart. Something worth boasting about. Worth busting a gut for. Every time a good person leaves the team it's like the brain losing a set of memories and brain cells. Even if the person is replaced the memories are still gone. From the person answering the e-mails to the person who maintains the database to person who designs your quality procedures. The people are the business. IBM's Director of Internet Technology puts it succinctly: 'The war is for talent and we want to have it'.

"The creative pool is finite"

The creative pool is finite. Consultancies are snapping up as much of it as possible so that they can charge you for renting it. The enlightened competition is trying desperately to find new ways of becoming the place to be and stay. This includes salary, stock options and profit share but the cultural snag is that it isn't just money that people want. They want their lives back.

You will need a wide range of perks. The standard list now includes casual dress, flexible hours, personal development training, employee entertainment, company product discounts, free food or beverages and telecommuting. Some businesses have gone further, including in their overall package circus performers, yachts, and finder fees for bringing in new people.

Don't become victim to what has been called the 'law of crappy people'.[62] It states that the standard of services, smiles and systems tends to fall to the ability level of the worst person in the business.

The electronic channel is the business face to the world. You cannot afford to have it culturally compromised. Respect and concern for the e-customer will come naturally from a business that respects every single one of its team. It's not just about the elite talent, it's about everyone. Without them there are no shopper Bots, the search engine won't work, your corporate look will stay trapped in 1994, and there will be no one to translate the gibberish into smart business decisions.

Hot news! Technology doesn't always work

This means that you need to figure out what you are going to do when it fails. What is the alternative? How to let the e-customer know? How do you find out what is going wrong? How do you put it right? How do you ensure that the e-customer does not lose all confidence when it fails for him?

This is a vital moment. The point at which trust can be deepened or diminished. It is not a point at which to skimp on good service. Don't penny-pinch when there are problems. Ensure that the greatest efforts are made to sooth the e-customer whenever there are difficulties. Even if it is expensive.

Too many companies attempt to cut costs even here. They hide the complaints-resolution process away from the home page. They fail to include it every time there is an error. Even if a telephone number is provided the first contact that is made on ringing is an automated-voice-response system. When technology has failed it shows poor judgement to try and let it correct that failure.

One of the challenges is that failure highlights the limitations of the non-human side of technology characteristics.

For a start, technology failure is often initially invisible or goes unnoticed by the business. When the system isn't working there are no 'intelligent, flexible, proactive' humans to notice. No do-gooder member of staff can let someone know so that the system can be changed or step into the breach and help the e-customer despite the problems.

It is also hugely lacking in empathy points – no one feels sorry for the 'poor, overworked computer' in the way they might feel sorry for the 'poor, overworked till clerk'. People don't tend to feel affection for computers (Apple owners apart) and they certainly don't understand what is happening when they don't work. Instead they will make an immediate and emotional decision that the system does not work and is therefore unreliable, poorly thought through and not worth using.

Going back to try again is unlikely to be the first option, since there is so much choice that there is no reason for the e-customer to use any service that is not measuring up. No geographical proximity arguments to change the actual preferences of the e-customer. No automatic footfall because the site is just on the high street.

People, on the whole, distrust computers. They may even envy them for all the features that they have that are an improvement over us. There is very certainly a competitive, comparative edge to many e-customer's use of the computer. And this happens even where the e-customer is experienced and enthusiastic. People deal with computers because the price of subjection is repaid in the advantages that they bring.

How to deal with technology failure

To overcome the failure, the first thing you need to do is assume it will happen. Yes – despite the best efforts of a 500-person programming

team the system will either stop working, produce errors or simply fail to meet the needs of the e-customer at some point. Recognizing that inevitability and the cost of systems failure should lead to a worthy conclusion that processes need to be put in place to allow the business to deal gracefully and dynamically with the problems.

So ask yourself the question: How would I know if the system was not working? There are four key ways of answering the question:

- First, implement systems that let you know what is happening with the system.

- Second, invite feedback from prospects and e-customers in a prominent manner.

- Third, have mystery shopping as a core, constant, daily part of your organization.

- Fourth, create alternatives that allow e-customers to still get the help that they need even when the core electronic offering is not available.

The error message that appears when a web page cannot be reached can itself be turned into a positive experience by showing something more creative than the infamous 'Error 404'.

Redherring.com, an online magazine, pitches its error message with grace and good humour as follows:

PLEASE PARDON OUR DUST!

WE ARE IN **PROCESS OF UPDATING** OUR SITE.

PLEASE CLICK THE BACK BUTTON ON YOUR BROWSER.

THANK YOU FOR YOUR PATIENCE.

This is written at a friendly, apologetic level that does much to re-establish trust with a credible explanation of why the link did not

work. The e-customer is left with the feeling that the site is working hard to improve content, with the natural result that not all links will work all of the time.

Dobedo.com, a cartoon-based online chat community, uses the following message when there are more serious faults:

IT'S A SERVER THING! **OH DEAR ...** LOOKS LIKE YOU HAVE CAUGHT US WITH **OUR SERVERS DOWN!** EVIL BOB HAS BEEN UP TO HIS USUAL **MISCHIEF** AND PUT A RIGHT SPANNER IN THE WORKS! REST ASSURED THAT OUR **DOBE-BOFFINS** ARE WORKING AT THIS VERY MOMENT TO REUNITE YOU WITH YOUR **BELOVED DOBEDO. NORMAL SERVICE** WILL BE REUNITING YOU VERY SHORTLY. DO BE HAPPY.

DO BE CHILLED. DOBEDO!

It is a message that actually builds on the richness of its offering which is based around the lives of a set of virtual island inhabitants. Evil Bob is given the blame for the problem and the efforts of technicians behind the scenes are made more prominent.

Sometimes the technology does not actually crash but fails because it does not give the e-customer what he wants. This is another moment of truth and one that many real and virtual stores do very little to resolve. Yet it is here that loyalty can be established that goes beyond price.

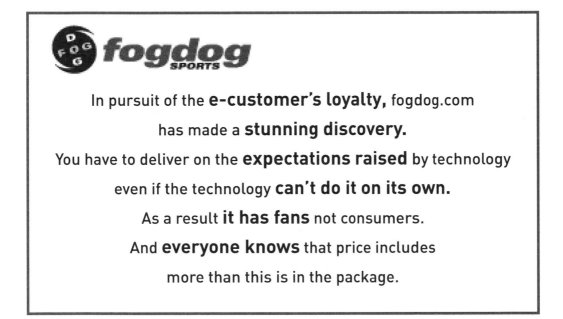

In pursuit of the **e-customer's loyalty,** fogdog.com
has made a **stunning discovery.**
You have to deliver on the **expectations raised** by technology
even if the technology **can't do it on its own.**
As a result **it has fans** not consumers.
And **everyone knows** that price includes
more than this is in the package.

The people at Fogdog.com understand this principle. They offer the quite wonderful 'Search Squad' that can be used free of charge by any of their actual or prospective e-customers. The e-customer simply fills out an easy-to-use form with a detailed description of the product and can expect a response within two to three business days.

No commission or mark-up is charged. Fogdog asks the e-customer to think of it as his very own personal shopper. And isn't that the way it should be? Certainly many of its own e-customers think so, including the following examples:

NOT ONLY DO I APPRECIATE THE HARD WORK YOU WENT THROUGH GETTING ME THIS JERSEY – I WOULD ALSO **LIKE TO COMMEND** YOU ON YOUR EFFORTS TO **KEEP ME INFORMED** DURING THE WHOLE PROCESS. YOU TOOK WHAT COULD HAVE BEEN A **HORRIBLE EXPERIENCE** (WITH THE DELAYS AND DISAPPOINTMENTS) AND **TURNED ME** INTO A LIFETIME FOGDOG CUSTOMER!

TODAY AT 14.00 WE RECEIVED THE MIZUNO-SPIKES. MANY THANKS **FOR THE FAST DELIVERY.** I WILL MAKE PUBLICITY FOR YOU HERE IN BELGIUM.

THANKS SO MUCH.

YOU'RE THE ONLY ONE WHO OFFERED TO HELP.

THANKS SO MUCH!!!

THANKS FOR YOUR EFFORTS. I WILL RETURN TO YOUR SITE IN THE FUTURE. YOUR WEBSITE AND RESPONSE GIVES ME **CONFIDENCE** IN YOUR SERVICES. MOST OF THE **OTHER WEBSITES** I TRAVELLED **DIDN'T SEEM** TO BE UP TO SPEED YET.

As a result of trying to help, fogdog.com can expect more than loyalty from Karen, Dennis, Mark and Eddy: it can expect passionate recommendation. It has shown them, and all who hear or read about it, enhanced trust in its desire and ability to help. In the end people still do business with people. People who care enough to prepare for every eventuality so that the e-customer 'has a nice day'.

SECTION

4

Back

""Real trust, real relationships, and real integrity""

to the beginning

Back to the beginning The conclusion takes us back to the
beginning: the e-customer.

As soon as you have managed to make him happy then it's back to the
beginning again. New ideas. New competitors. New fads. And new
opportunities. It's not really possible to have an end to a book that
argues that business should be an endless value exchange with the
e-customer.

" Be the friend that

The whole business world needs a good slap around the back of the head. Someone holding its head down shouting, 'What is that? What do you think about that?'

So open up your heart and hear this.

Twenty-one principles to win hearts and wallets

There is no joy to be found in doing a half a job and there's very little money either. You need to **get into the mind of the real e-customer**. And he's legion, multiple, distinctive, and ever-changing.

You can't force him to feed. He's hungry but not for tasteless slop. Electronic channels need to **open up all six senses** to an improved world. They exist because of the relentless need of the inventive to build a better way. Networks were built to connect. The internet was put together to combine the thoughts and research of one group in a way that did not depend on the centre. If the channels do not change the world then we should shut them down. Turn them off.

Just stop throwing away the legacy of the e-generations. Believe that what you are offering is worth more than it costs to provide. **Make your profits the honest way**. Offer the e-customer real value and he will come back tomorrow, teach him it's free and he will expect it for a lifetime. Create stuff that the e-customer will appreciate and value – something more than just an alternative use of his money.

Adopt the hacker's perspective. Build things that matter. Give back to the e-customer. View waste as evil. Expand your mind. **Let in dangerous**

the e-customer
cannot live without „

thoughts. Anything is possible in this post-DNA world. Everything will happen. You must think of everything.

The e-customer will never stop wanting it all. So make the desirable feasible. Turn the **impossible into the profitable** and be sought after. The e-customer will come to you if you have what he wants before everybody else. If you always have it first then trust can start to deliver supernormal profits.

Be the friend that the e-customer cannot live without. Present loving arms that **hide the technology**. Robo-Nanny. Techno-Host. Welcome him in. Serve him and turn his demands into revenue. Match his whingeing with your wisdom. Align yourself to his desire to be smarter with less effort and experience infinite growth.

See and serve your e-customer multi-dimensionally. Link the real world and the virtual world with bridges that offer handrails and an easy gradient. **Let the diversity of the e-customer flood into your organization**. Respond with a team that can use its expertise and experience to represent the e-customer. Designing for his priorities, his eyes, his ears, his world, and using his tone.

Free agency. Choice. Accountability. Life-affirming values. They are the most effective tools for coping with the legion of personalities that arrive at your electronic door. Don't depend on convergence to allow you to limit the playlist. Do you know the e-customer? If you sing it, I can play it. You will never guess what they all want so **let them make their own world**. Guide them to it. Play the part of mentor.

Don't rush on the first date. There is plenty of time to pop, sparkle and slide messages past his eyes and into his brain. First he has to be open to the new ideas and most e-customers aren't ready when they are acclimatizing themselves to your little place. A new world for him. Take it easy.

If it isn't usable then it isn't useful. If it isn't useful you won't be able to give it away. Oops! Did you try and give it away? **Get to the point**. Make it clear how you can help to solve his problems. Say it in less than 20 words. And then keep on saying it through the design of every picture, paragraph and pointer.

Keeping the blindfold on

Don't spread yourself too thin or lay it on too thick. You really cannot be the best at everything that the e-customer wants. It may be easier to get it from you than clicking to the competition. It may be more reliable. **Unclutter your rhetoric**. Tidy up your offer. It is better to be known for a little of something than a lot of nothing.

Make sure that the team understands all 2001 dialects of gibberish. The stuff you don't understand can still kill you. **Keeping the blindfold on won't stop the bullets**. Learn a smattering yourself so that you can at least follow the conversation. Having smart interpreters in alien worlds is good but relying on them for every nuance is foolish. The faster the pace of change the more you will need to know. Keep the learning habit and get past the addiction to the way it was.

Being afraid of what is to come or greedily trying to get your piece of net pie is insufficient. It will not sustain you in the hard times to come. When the flurry of easy money has evaporated, when the world starts to see things as they really are, **ignorance, fear and covetousness will be unmasked**. Maybe you will get away with it but there is a better way to live.

The e-customer is returning to his profoundest desires *and* his most outlandish wishes. He wants the real thing. More than the real thing, he wants experiences. To find a life. He does not believe that life can be bought or that the purpose of life is in celebrating its pointlessness. He is moving beyond modernism and post-modernism to a post-ironic peak. **He aims to get a life through living**. Helping the e-customer get connected to the world is a business worth being in.

When he gets mad simply **channel his passion into a relationship** with your service. His anger is not something he wants. It is frustration caused by not

won't stop the bullets

getting what he wants. He raises his voice when he feels that he is not being heard. Give him alternatives and bond.

Rise above the lists. Above the possible providers. The e-customer owns himself and will choose his friends. Be his best mate. Really! Work for him and make sure you get paid for the effort. **Don't take or be taken for granted**. You earn your right to be considered worthwhile just as he pays for the right to have your help. If the exchange is good for both of you then you have a chance of staying together.

Don't build your future plans on the successful flukes of the past. If you can't remember why your business is successful then your e-customer will eventually forget you. **Avoid becoming irrelevant or upgradeable**. Keep the focus on the simple benefits that you bring into his life. Change the style and substance of the stuff that you do for him as his lifestyle and expectations change.

Keep it real. Get in among the crowds. Glad-hand and listen. Change yourself, your team, your systems and your business. It's a relationship thing. The e-customer wants **real trust, real relationships and real integrity**. Anything less than transparency in intent and implementation will create suspicion. There are no walls, there are no secrets. It's an open world.

Unshrink the people. **Let their personalities out to fill up the place with humanity**. It's the most valuable, priceless, attractive part. The network gives the world back its interaction. What else is being multimedia, two-way, and real time about? People: hundreds of millions, then billions, until the air is used to connect every last one of us. Be part of making that work better and enjoy the ride.

So that's it. My impassioned plea to do more. To think further. To believe that what you can offer is more than exists. That your life's work can make money by making the world a better place. **Build your kingdom where the e-customer has his heart.**

The internet has a spirit. Connecting people creates innovative power. It has a culture. An approach and ethos. It is possible to make money without understanding the way the stream is flowing, but it could all be so much more successful. My fear is that too few will settle for survival of the average rather than use electronic channels for what they exist to achieve.

Be different.

Inspire

the e-customer.

notes

1   Chris Riley, Wieden & Kennedy, ' Has the e-customer changed or it is our understanding of the e-customer that has changed?' Customer of the future, GBN World View Meeting, New York, 13–15 October 1999.

2   Richardson, Cheryl, Take Time for Your Life, Broadway Books, 1999.

3   'Like dreams statistics are a form of wish fulfilment', Jean Baudrillard (French semiologist), Cool Memories, 1987.

4   'Traditional market research can tell you you what your e-customers like, and what they don't, but it won't necessarily tell you can do a better job of meeting their needs and winning their loyalty' Vincent de Veau, 'Consumer journeys', AerLingus flight magazine, July–August 1999'.

5   Field of Dreams, the 1989 Kevin Costner film, is based on the 1982 book, Shopless Joe, by W.P. Kinsella. It tells the story of an Iowa corn farmer who hears voices that tell him to build a baseball diamond in his fields; he does, and the famous (but disgraced) Chicago black sox come. (For more see fieldofdreamsmoviesite.com).

6   The animated animal craze continued with hamsterdance.com, mahirdance.com, homerdance.com.

7   The USA soccer team has an overall record of only 43% losses, but in the World Cup this increases to 70% (rsssf.com).

8   But positive and negative experiences both personal and shared, will shape attitudes thereafter. Successful merchants will be those who learn to send the appropriate signals, so that the buying public can surf among the sharks.' Sirkka Jarvenpaa and Stefano Frazioli. 'Surfing among the sharks: how to gain trust in cyberspace mastering information management '. Financial Times, 15 March 1999.

9   In the world of cyberspace everywhere is an exit. You have the capacity to bail out at any point, and an enormous number of people do.' Paco Underhill in article by Erica Good: 'The on-line consumer? Tough, impatient and gone in a blink', New York Times, 22 September 1999.

10   Eastor Su in letter to Fortune, 12 June 1999.

11   There were 21,287 business failures in the UK in 1999.

12   In a flash, Nicholas Hall was hit with the idea, startupfailures.com – 'The Place for Bouncing Back'. It's the first community focused on supporting individuals that have recently gone through or are going through the experience of a start-up failure. 'Our purpose is to take the stigma out of failing and to help you recover quickly from a failure and get back into the game and in action. The only true true failure is never trying.'

13   Mug (v.) meaning to assault or threaten with the intent to rob. The director of a UK bank once asked his consultancy how he could mug the punters, more effectively with the internet.

14   Jakob Neilson said 'Avoid using Virtual gimmicks (say a virtual shopping mall) that emulates the physical world. The goal of web design is to be better that reality. If you ask users to "Walk around a mall", "you are putting your user interface in the way of that goal.

15 This is why our e-customer diary (www.maverickandstrong.com) does not focus solely on net shopping.

16 Erich Fromm points out in his book To Have or To Be Continuum, 1996.

17 From the episode Wild Barts Can't Be Broken.

18 During the 1960s, the US Department of Defense focused its research on the development of a non-centralized network. The original ARPANET had four sites: University of California at Los Angeles, University of California at Santa Barbara, Stanford Research Institute and the University of Utah. In the 1970s, it kept on growing to over 100.000 sites and was relaced in 1989 by the FSFNET (dei.isep.ipp.pt/docs/arpa-Contents.html).

19 There are many fine internet histories on the net itself. Use internet.about.com to find one to read.

20 According to a representative survey in the USA of 500 people by decisionanalyst.com.

21 Do as the UK bank Woolwich who showed the problems of waiting in line for personal service at a real-world branch: you wait many minutes, but then are not recognized.

22 Check out the web cam at bbc.co.uk/radio1.

23 McKinsey & Co./Solomon Smith Barney Etail Economic Study 2000.

24 Bain & Co., 2000.

25 Like the Connect, Find and Shop service from quixi.com that targets the 15–20 million wireless consumers who continually depend on new and innovative ways to get things done. Customers will have access to a live helper 24 hours a day, 7 days a week for $19.95 per month and $2.50 a purchase. 'We like to think of quixi as the first manufacturer of time', says Evan Marwell, co-funder, quixi. 'We make more time for mobile multi-taskers to help increase their personal productivity. We do this by offering valuable, timesaving services that can be accessed while on the go, through our live human helpers.'

26 MSN.com (Microsoft Network) has said it will include the option to contact a real person along with its regular web search service. Instead of typing in a search term and wading through page after page of possibly unhelpful returns, just click on a button and a helpful expert calls up and answers the question.

27 $50 of software creates a pseudonymous digital identity, called a nym, that lets you surf the web, send e-mail, chat, and use newsgroups without leaving a trace. Freedom routes your data through a network of 150 servers; Zero-Knowledge never knows its source or destination. Your identity remains secret, and personal information will not make its way into the wrong hands. Not just for the paranoid, Freedom offers peace of mind in the nosy, invasive world of the web.

28 Estimated internet users in 2000: world total 332.73 million, Africa 2.77 million, Asia/Pacific 75.5 million, Europe 91.82 million, Middle East 1.90 million, Canada and the USA 147.48 million, South America 13.19 million. That means that the entire internet universe, and its 2 billion pages, still only includes 4.5% of the world's population!

29   Daniel Nettle & Suzanne Romaine, Vanishing Voices, Oxford University Press, 2000.

30   Helen Kirwan-Taylor, Management Today, June 2000.

31   Consider the experience of petsmart.com where each member was provided with 10 MB of free web space for their personal use with an easy-to-remember web address under the main brands domain to help enhance it and extend reach. To date, thousands have signed up for free home pages, using them to show off their pets or to sell everything from pet-training services to home-baked dog biscuits. On average those with home pages receive 55 page views per month.

32   For several years now, media executives have been trying to figure out what form of media is being cannibalized by new options such as the PC and the internet. Evidence suggests that instead of cannibalization, consumers are simply fitting 30 hours of activity into 24-hour days. A study by MTV Network and Viacom, 2000.

33   Teenagers even have a language of their own, for example POS meaning Parent Over Shoulder for their online conversations. Article by Louise Kehoe, FT.

34   Swedish site, dobedo.com, was inspired by TV shows like The Simpsons and created by Richard Kylberg and Magnus Leijonberg. It offers e-customers a novel chat service that allows them to create their own animated cartoon characters to represent them while chatting. This not only promises more bizarre internet conversations than ever before, but also means that chat users will be able to reach new levels of emotional expression.

35   Allan & Barbara Pease, Why Men Don't Listen and Women Can't Read Maps, Welcome Rain, 2000.

36   Ernst & Young online survey of 1,200 internet users, April 2000.

37   Bruskin/Goldring survey of 1,016 adults who have internet access for Clinique, October 1998.

38   Taylor Nelson Sofres Intersearch survey of 400 women conducted for Shop2u.co, May 1999.

39   PC Data survey of 2,812 internet users August 1999.

40   Harris survey of 500 online women for Procter & Gamble and women.com, 1997.

41   NetSmart, September 1999.

42   Cyber Dialogue, 2000.

43   NPD Online Research.

44   DSA Group, 1998.

45   Ernst & Young.

46   Gnutella, like Napster, enables sharing of digitally recorded music (MP3) but with more anonymity and resistance to legislative controls.

47   As an example of the work of WAI, look at open.gov.uk and ask why all sites don't have electronic keyboard short-cuts. Really! Why not?

48 In another similar incident, Nike lost control of its home page to a group of activists demanding 'global justice'. 'Global Justice is coming – prepare now!' the erstwhile Nike.com site read, directing surfers to the website of an Australian organization called S–11. The group urged supporters to protest at the September 2000 World Economic Forum in Melbourne, Australia.

49 e-Marketer.com, 2000.

50 If you are stuck with dowdy monchrome internet phones at the moment, it may seem unlikely that you are dealing with a revolution. But already in Japan, with over 11 million connected e-customers, unmodified full-colour websites are being presented on mobile phones complete with sound and graphics. The technology encourages development because it just uses a slimmed down version of HTML (cHTML). Content, the key to any channel, is therefore guaranteed, rich, and diverse.

51 Winning in Mobile E-Markets, TIMElabs, January 2000.

52 By 2003 Europeans will outnumber Americans by nearly two to one when it comes to accessing the net by cell phone.

53 Forrester, January 2000.

54 According to the International e-customer Service Association (ICSA) and e-Satisfy.com.

55 Entertainment Weekly.

56 Just make sure that the e-customer can easily unsubscribe!

57 Tokyomotortrenz.com is a store in San Francisco of Honda accessories where you can find an interesting service. It customizes any Nokia 5100 or 6100 series phone, it dismantles handsets and replaces the works with tricked-out parts, iridescent covers with glow-in-the-dark backs, rainbow-patterned buttons, showy antennae and souped-up battery packs.

58 This stuff isn't new (apple.com offered such facilities from the mid 1990s) but the e-customer loves to demonstrate his differerences. Software from Neoplanet.com is already allowing e-customers to alter the way that their browsers look. Microsoft.com have hinted that they will provide similar facilities for the complete operating system. The company has said it plans to add new speech, annotation and other natural-language capabilities to its Windows-user interface in the not-too-distant future.

59 Colin 'Gabriel' Hatcher, Cyber Angels Internet Safety Organization.

60 'You've got mayhem', Wired, September 2000.

61 A survey conducted by the Association of MBAs found that 42% envisage working independently.

62 Marc Andresson, founder of netscape.com and loud.com.

INDEX